# Economic Life of Nomads in India

A.T. Thomas

GRP
GLOBAL RESEARCH PUBLICATIONS
NEW DELHI (INDIA)

First Published - 2011

ISBN: 978-81-89630-42-3



*Published by*

**GLOBAL RESEARCH PUBLICATIONS**
4800/24, 1st Floor, Ansari Road
Darya Ganj, New Delhi-110002 (India)
Phone : 23245225. Fax : 91-11-23272135
E-mail: globalresearchpublications@gmail.com, grpindia@vsnl.net

# CONTENTS

# FOREWORD

We are proud to be part of the development process of gypsies in Tamil Nadu. This book is the result of an action oriented research undertaken by Fr.A.T. Thomas sdb, the Additional Principal and Professor of Economics at Sacred Heart College, Tirupattur, Vellore District, and more as a field activist among the people of Narikoravas for the past nine years.

Narikoravas are the most disadvantaged section of the people of Tamil Nadu. Behind the smiling exterior of a fast growing economy today in India, lie the tears and tragedies of Narikoravas who lead trampled lives. Theirs is a story of living on the brinks in every sense of the word as they still eke out a living as gypsies. They were once travellers on the high roads of freedom, crafting their own destinies as hunters, gatherers, traders, hawkers and craftsmen, but exist today in the no-man's-land of the settled world. Nevertheless they persist. The major issues which confront them are poverty, illiteracy and discrimination.

Being a nomadic community, the Narikoravas face extreme discrimination in society. Being highly unorganized as a community, has further weakened their voices against discrimination. Their culture, a very live and constantly changing one, lacks any kind of documentation and their language still exists as a creole.

The need to integrate the community is of utmost importance. And so is the need to educate the common populace about the Narikoravas on their culture and tradition. They do not want handouts but opportunities to create wealth. These are some of the issues that are addressed in this research work.

The Salesian Organization has taken many initiatives for the development of these people and it invites people of goodwill to join in this noble endeavor so that we can see a day when all the Narikoravas will be fully integrated into the mainstream of the country.

As I congratulate the author once again on his thought-provoking and wonderful work with commonsense solutions to their interminable problems, the readers are called to involve themselves in the process of integrating the gypsies of Tamil Nadu.

**August 2011**

**Rev. Dr. Jayapalan Raphael SDB**
**Salesian Provincial, Chennai**

# PREFACE

This book is on a group of ostracized people that still live on the fringes of society and it is a product of long time commitment and intellectual spadework. While there are important issues of assessment and evaluation of this nomadic group, the primary focus of this book is to give greater conscientization and proactive approach to their problems. Effectiveness of governmental action can take a back seat as long as there is vote bank politics which is typical of Indian society. This book is an eye-opener in every sense of the word as it touches on every facet of their daily drudgery that goes on without whine or whimper.

The world over the theorem of growth is basically a function of saving and investment. In India there is a third variable, politics. The price of sop politics has in the least mitigated the poverty of the hapless people. Hence the author likes to harp on inclusive growth that is at the very heart of economic growth and poverty reduction.

Narikoravas of Tamil Nadu, and Vellore district in particular, who have been living at the periphery of the society needs to be brought to the mainstream that calls for visible policy interventions to extricate them from the shackles of penury as their income and expenditure patterns have not changed for the better during the study period. The test of this programme is ultimately the quality of service at the cutting edge level. India of 2011 may not have found its dubious place among the most corrupt nations of the world, but it has made the life of ordinary citizens that the politicians call 'aam aadmi' a living hell in the land of his dreams. And

Narikoravas have been the greatest losers. Their development story has been bumpy and inconsistent with the offer of few occasional freebies that has been in the spotlight with the present state dispensation. But the new challenge is to shake off the trauma of societal indifference and winning their hearts to gain a 'place in the sun' at the earliest.

This book attempts to spell out a tailor- made strategies taking into consideration their background, culture and types of trade and thus leading to their emancipation within democratic polity.

First and foremost, I extend my sincere appreciation and thanks to my Guide and Supervisor Dr. K.S.S. Uduman Mohideen, Professor and Head, Dept. of Economics, (Retd.), University of Madras for having graciously accepted to guide me in the PhD programme for past three years. I deeply appreciate his ready availability, meticulous corrections, intellectual acumen and tireless work that he has manifested during my research period.

My special thanks go to Fr. K.M. Jose, the Rector and Rev. Dr. C. Antontyraj, the Principal who have egged me on to complete this work at the earliest with their unstinted support, Fr. Xavier P, the Administrator for his generous financial backup and every member of the Salesian Community of the College for their constant encouragement.

I wish to place on record my gratitude to the members of the Doctoral Committee for their valuable suggestions and critical comments for fine-tuning my thesis.

My special thanks are to Dr. L. Venkatachalam, Associate Professor of MIDS, Chennai, and Dr. A.J. Christopher, Associate Professor, Dept. of Social Work, Sacred Heart College (Autonomous), Tirupattur, for their invaluable help in data analysis.

I place on record my sincere gratitude to Rev. Dr. Leonard, S.J, the former Principal of Loyola College, Chennai, Rev. Dr. P.P. George, SDB, former Principal of my college, Dr. S. Bhakthavatsala Bharathi, Associate Professor, Puducherry Institute of Linguistic and Culture, Mr. P. Annamalai, I.A.S, Commissioner, Most Backward Class and Denotified

Communities, Chennai, Dr. A. Xavier Susairaj, my colleague in the department, and Dr. Karuppiah, HOD of Sociology Dept., University of Madras, for their support in providing valuable materials and constant encouragement on the study of Narikoravas.

It is my pleasure to thank the Principal of Madras School of Social Work, the Director of Folklore Institute at Nungambakkam, (Chennai) and the Director of Folklore Resource and Research Centre, St. Xavier's College, Palayamkottai, for their kind cooperation in providing me help in collecting literature pertaining to my research study.

I owe a debt of gratitude to Ancheneyan, K. Manoj Kumar and G. Sudhakar who backed me up with data collection and computer operations. Besides I am ever grateful to the UGC for supporting me financially to undertake this pioneering research work.

The inspiration to undertake this project was drawn from the Narikorava friends themselves, particularly from Idaya Nagar, Tirupatur, for whom I continue to work since several years. Their willing and spontaneous cooperation in data collection is ever remembered with love and gratitude. I firmly believe that my efforts at this research will pitchfork bold initiatives to alleviate their misery at the earliest.

I am convinced that the adequacy of this work is due to the helps I have received from all those named and many others for whom I simply cannot take this space to name.

Lastly, my sincere thanks go to Global Research Publications, New Delhi for coming forward to publish my thesis in record time.

**A.T. Thomas**

# 1

# INTRODUCTION

Modernization and development process have everywhere been a threat to the cultural identity and dignity of the marginalized people with vast diverse ethnicities and languages, even in countries such as India where there is official policy of protection and promotion of their welfare. Among the oppressed, it is the nomadic tribes in particular who are the most vulnerable when change overtakes them. More than others, they are under threat of being assimilated into the bottom of the social strata, as even now they are being displaced from their traditional base in the name of an unacceptable 'development' from whose benefits they are alienated.[1]

As India sprints on a fast track of economic growth, it needs to restructure this development pattern if it has to reach the people who need it most, like the ones that live on the fringes of society. But the structural violence that such 'development' inflicts on its victims is only part of the indignity to which they are subjected. For there is also an accompanying cultural hegemony that subverts identity, and in doing so undermines the very cultural resources which such groups would have collectively found in their tribal identity to mobilize against this dominance.

In an ever-changing globalised world with the dominant economic and political systems penetrating the remotest areas of local societies, isolationism can only be pious wish rather than a social reality. There are no longer any islands of cultural forms in a world where 'human ways of life increasingly influence, dominate, parody, translate and subvert one another (Clifford 1990; 22). For the inevitable linkages and interdependence in a rapidly integrating world system only accentuate the tension between 'local voices' and global forces.'[2] And yet there is a yawning gap between what is obviously accepted and practised today in India even after sixty years of independence, particularly with regard to these nomadic people like Narikoravas who still languish in the periphery of development process.

## GYPSIES: THEIR ROOTS

The popular conception of gypsies is shrouded in mystery and the scientific accounts of their origins reflect some degree of uncertainty as well. Whatever their true origin is (if indeed they come from a single place) has been long debated question.

"It appears that the term 'gypsy' is a corruption of "Egyptian" reflecting the widespread belief during the Middle Ages that these people were of Egyptian origin. One of their major camps was known as "Little Egypt" because the locals believed the people were from Egypt. However the connection to Egypt is all but completely non-existent. It is most likely that they originated in northern India, in the Punjab region, an area between India and Pakistan as we know them today. Another interpretation claims that they acquired the name "gypsies" from their settlement in the Greek Peloponneseus near a village named "Gyppe."[3] These people fairly and consistently call themselves Rom or Roma.

Table-1 shows that the gypsy diaspora is global, particularly in the western hemisphere and their number is only a wild guesswork. Besides, those who call themselves so, are known by different names in the East.

"The term "gypsies" used here, refers to various ethnic groups including Roma, Sinti, Manouches, Kal, Gitani, Yenish, Roamanichals, Boyash, Ashkali, Travellers,etc. In Western Europe (the United Kingdom, Spain and France) and in certain areas of Russia, Asia and America, the term "gypsy" or the equivalent "Tsigane", "Gitano", "Cigbny", "Tsyganye" and others is more appropriate. In Central and Eastern Europe, the term "Roma" is widely used when referring to these populations, as for many Roma and Sinti, the term "gypsy" has negative connotations, because it is linked to widespread negative and paternalistic stereotypes regarding them."[4]

The Roma are considered as the descendants of Rajputs and Jats of North India who by accidents of history were forced to migrate to foreign lands during the Muslim invasion in 10th to 13th centuries A.D and are now leading a non-sedentary life. Their forefathers lived as Hindus in Western India, which included old Sind, Punjab, Rajasthan, Maharastra, Gujarath etc. In spite of the long break with their country of origin, India, whom they still call Baro Than (the land of their ancestors), they still speak a language which has Sanskrit base and is akin to the language spoken in the Greater Punjab of Alberuni's description now comprising of Punjab, Haryana, Himachal Pradesh, Delhi and the adjacent parts of Rajasthan.[5]

Hence "it is not clear if the Indian region is the primitive place of origin of gypsy culture or may be an intermediate step in a more complex migration."[6]

On the authority of Grierson, the author of the monumental work "Linguistic Survey of India" it can be said emphatically that these Roma (the so-called gypsies of Europe, Russia, Americas etc) are in no way connected with the so-called gypsies of India. The word gypsy used in dealing with gypsy tribes of India is employed in its purely conventional sense of vagrant and should not be taken as suggesting their any connection whatsoever with the Roma. In fact there are no gypsies in India. But all over India, there are nomadic castes or tribes who are gypsy-like in their mode of life, habits, trades and character but they use the dialects of the districts whence they come or where they are found. They also speak secret languages differing entirely from one another -made up jargons of various sorts and all resembling far less Romani language than Hindi dialects do. None of these jargons can be the origin of gypsy language. Moreover, the Roma hate to be called gypsies.[7]

**Table 1**
**Gypsies in the World**

| *Country* | *Population size* |
|---|---|
| Turkey | From 3,00,000 to 5,000,000 |
| Romania | Official census: 535,250 |
| Spain | From 6,00,000 to 1,500,000 |
| France | From 5,00,00 (official est.) to 1,300,000 |
| United States of America | 1,000,000 (data from gypsy organization) |
| Hungary | Official census 205,720 |
| Russia | Official census: 2002:183,000 |
| Brazil | From 678,000 to 9,00,000 |
| Bulgaria | Official census from 370,908 to 8,00,000 |
| Serbia | Official census: 108,193 |
| Slovakia | From 92,500 to 550,000 |
| Ukraine | Official census from 48,000 to 400,000 |
| Bosnia & Herzegovina | Official census from 8,864 to 4,00,000 |
| Greece | From 2,00,000 to 350,000 |
| Argentina | 3,00,000 |
| Czech Republic | From 11,746 to 3,00,000 |
| Macedonia | From 53,879 to 260,000 |
| Moldavia | Official census (2004) 12,280 to 150,000 |
| Croatia | Official census (2001) 9,463 to 131,000 |
| Germany | From 110,000 to 130,000 |
| Albania | From 1,300 to 12,000 |
| Iran | 110,000 |
| Italy | 90,000 to 110,000 |
| Canada | 80,000 |
| Colombia | 79,000 |
| Portugal | 40,000 |
| Poland | From 15,000 to 50,000 |

*Source*: Wikipedia, 2009.

Roma denotes them as a nation. This is the name, which the First World Romani Congress adopted for them. They are also known by other names in different countries of the world, which again point out to their Indian origin. They are also called by other names derived from their main name 'Rom.'[8]

The history of gypsies prior to 1417 - when they emerged from Hungary and crossed the frontiers of German - is almost shrouded in darkness. Scattered proofs have been found of their residence at an early date in the Slavic countries and in the island of Cyprus but all else is conjecture. Thus Grellmann has placed their departure from India at the time of Timur, an idea more fully worked out by Rienzi and Heister, who assume that they were employed by Timur as spies and foragers and that they were afterwards carried further west by the Turks in the same capacity. There is nothing to be found in the history of Timur for or against it.

What is known about the Sinti and Roma is that they arrived in Germany in the late 1400's after a series of migrations, which brought them from Northern India through Persia, Asia Minor and Greece, the Balkan and Slavic States, the Austria and Germany. Along the way, they converted to Christianity and acquired a wide range of stereotypes including 'accomplices to the crucifixion', thieves, practitioners of magic arts, beggars etc. Their itinerant lifestyles, non-conventional behaviors and mystical image brought them under government suspicion from the early Middle Ages on. "They had undergone a series of persecutions during this period. Since the nation states were being formed, and social control and settlements were being emphasised, gypsies started to look different; it was no longer just the colour of their skin, their odd-looking clothing, the mysterious aura surrounding them, but their way of life which looked suspicious and frowned upon."[9]

Thus, a process of 'criminalisation' of gypsy way of life was set in motion as they were accused of being parasites. In the centuries that followed, expulsion orders were gradually issued by most European states. "Enlightened Despotism" tried to wipe out the gypsy culture and customs to give them citizenship rights, which at least interrupted the persecutions. But this attempt at forced "civilization" was a fiasco and caused sufferings that led to their extermination altogether.

In 1933 any residue of tolerance went overboard and in 1936 the "Wohnlager" was built, places where gypsies had to live under police control and they also had to submit to biological experiments, beginning with sterilization followed by deportations. It would be hard to ascertain the total number of gypsies who died due to Nazi persecutions; the number varies around 250,000 to 500,000.

In recent decades, persecution of these people has not died down. Being pushed out or marginalised, episodes of racism and blatant discrimination are the order of the day making their destiny as bleak as ever. They were fairly and consistently defined as 'stateless wanderers', a threat to the moral order and a burden upon society.

Many now believe that the 'Roma' was a group from North West India, mainly low-caste Sudra, who migrated to Europe and North Africa via the Iranian plateau around 1050 A.D. The roots of their culture can be sought in India. Moreover, many other influences are interwoven into culture, and over centuries of migration, gypsies have come into strict contact with many people taking on, their customs and habits.

Many legends suggest that they were banished. Today, the 'Roma' are dispersed into three categories, based on geography, the Rom (European Roma) Lom (specifically the Armenians) and Dom (specifically Iran). These terms are phonetically correspondent to Sanskrit's 'domba' or modern Indian terms like dom or dum.[10] In Sanskrit domba means man of low caste living by singing and music. In modern Indian tongues, the corresponding words have similar or related meanings. There are references to the Dom as musicians from the sixteenth century. The Dom still exists in India; they are nomads who do a number of jobs like basket making, smithing, metalworking, scavenging, music-making etc. Not surprisingly many people have leapt on a Dom theory of origins of the gypsies.[11]

Modern scholars no longer doubt that the gypsies originated in India, but many problems concerning ethnic group, social class, and the period of their earliest migrations are still confusing with inconsistencies in documentation. The assumption that all the gypsies scattered throughout Europe have descended from one parent stock meets with little contradiction. Both of these beliefs are the outcome of the investigation of their language.

## NOMADISM IN THE WORLD

The term "nomads" means different things to different scholars. On one hand some scholars have defined nomads as all those leading a mobile way of life independent of its economic specificity while other scholars have described nomads as extensive and mobile pastoralists who either have nothing to do with agriculture, or who are occupied with agriculture to a limited degree in the capacity of a secondary and supplementary activity. However, the first notion is gradually going out of use.

One needs to understand the concept of nomadism while we rediscover the place of Narikoravas in the world of nomadism. Nomadism is as old as the history of mankind. Besides, the compulsions of nature and search for food, quest for knowledge and the explorations of the unknown regions have led people to move from one place to another and interact with different groups of people. Most of the South Asian countries still tend to consider nomadism as an anachronism, result of laziness or criminal tendencies and an obvious sign of backwardness, surprisingly unscathed by the development process around them. Nomadism is seldom understood here as a major risk-spreading strategy where the vagaries of weather often led to partial or total crop failure where agriculture may not be sustainable on any account. Nomadism must be seen as logical response to scattered resources. Herding, gathering, hunting, nomadic servicing and petty trade constitute rational, practical and viable alternative to wage labour, settled agriculture and act as major buffers against unpredictability and risk, enabling the creation and sustenance of efficient economies. "Sociologists articulate that before the advent of transportation and communication, mobile groups served as the useful adjuncts to sedentary societies. As occupational groups of hunters, trappers, blacksmiths, basket weavers and entertainers like puppeteers, acrobats, fortune-tellers, singers, and dancers, the nomads shared a symbiotic relationship with settled people. In return for their services, they were allowed to squat on the village commons and use resources such as water or pasture lands for grazing their cattle till they moved on to their next dera (settlement)."[12]

The word 'nomad' is of Greek origin ('nomas-ados' meaning roaming about for pasture) and it is referred to the people who lead a migratory life, have no fixed abode, tend and raise cattle[13]. The term now has a wider application and it refers to those people who habitually and repeatedly shift their non-permanent habitat in search of subsistence. 'The repeated movements of nomads from one place to another are based on realistic considerations and stipulated direction, and are focused around certain centres of operation for obtaining the livelihood and characteristically have a definite end points of their movement and point of return".[14]

There are an estimated 30-40 million nomads in the world. Many cultures have been traditionally nomadic, but traditional nomadic behaviour is increasingly rare in industralised countries.

Nomads have been variously classified. Bacon classifies them as true nomads, semi-nomads and semi-sedentary. According to him, true nomads are those who dwell round the year in non-permanent dwellings and who practice no agriculture. Semi-nomads are those who plant a few crops at their base camps before moving out on seasonal migrations but they normally live in portable dwellings round the year. The semi-sedentary live in permanent villages during a part of the year and wander for the rest of the period. Hence going by the common traits of the Narikoravas, the researcher was nudged to conclude that they are semi-nomads of Tamil Nadu.[15]

Scant attention has been given to these and other starkly poor nomadic groups in India. Though the bibliography given at the end of this paper is rather bulky, a careful examination of it reveals that material on India is too thin and most of it is in the form of small papers. In fact South Asia has the world's largest nomadic population. In India alone, roughly 7 per cent of the contemporary population is nomadic and consists of about 500 different communities forming substantial portion of the population. Economically, culturally and demographically, it is thus incorrect to consider nomads as 'fringe groups' (Ratnager 1991). In sheer numbers, India has the world's largest nomadic population, and nowhere else is there such variety of creatures systematically 'herded' nor is the diversity of peripatetic professions to be matched. Of these, mobile herders, foragers and peripatetics stand out.[16]

Nomadism is not seen here primarily in relation to specific forms of social and political organization or worldview. It is considered foremost as a strategy that permits and enhances access to resources, which can lead to specific forms of socio-political organization. Nomadism is also seen as a resilient, rational response to variety of ecological, economic, political and social circumstances that corrode every effort to enhance income and consequently degrade ones daily life.

## MYTHS ON NOMADISM

The myth on nomadism may be even older than the myth of the "noble savage". By the middle of the fifth century B.C in the writing of Herodotus, the Father of history in Western culture, idealized descriptions of nomad, as may be found in Ephorous. This myth was carried over into the Middle Ages. Philosophers and travelers have influenced each other. Many source and ideas on them were misinformed; at the same time there has been a great desire and search for such misinformation about nomadism. Apart from its light side, the myth of the nomad also has darker side in which a nomad is perceived almost as the devil incarnate. In China, the Confucians simply despised the barbarian nomads, considering them incapable of following civilized way of life. In the West, both before and after Jordanes, believed the Huns were descendants of evil spirits and witches. (Getica 121) From the time of biblical prophets, the view of nomads was excessively savage and wild and God chastised them in particular fashion. This was the view held by early Christian authors. Attila was described as the "scourge of God". In the Middle Ages similar notions were very widespread and popular. They were often included in the register of disasters, which listed among other things, cholera and plague.

But the dark side of their life remained the same. It has been used more than once in colonial and even post-colonial times by politicians as a means to manipulate public opinion.

The phenomenon of nomadism consists basically of

- Not as a specialized occurrence but as a very widespread one existing all over the world except in Australia and to a certain degree in America.
- In its role of linking different societies and cultures.
- Not only in its economic but also in its social and historical specificity.[17]

It is interesting to note that nomads could never exist on their own without the outside world and its non-nomadic societies, with their different economic systems. Indeed a nomadic society could only function while the outside world not only existed but also allowed for those reactions from it-reactions which were economic, social, political, cultural, in a word, a multi-faceted response which ensured that the nomads remained nomads.

## NOMADISM IN INDIA

As there is a variety of nomadism across the world, India with its multiethnic landscape, presents a unique array of nomadism connected with its ancient civilization. "The nomads moving in the villages, towns and even cities represent a unique institution of this country and they are tremendous pressure."[18] There was a time this term was referred to pastoral nomads alone. But this notion is changing as more information about the migratory groups is becoming available and as they tend to assert their due rights in the society. Now not only the term has wider connotation but also several supportive terms are being used along with it to distinguish one set of nomads from others.

In order to systematize our information, we may take a minimal definition of nomads as those who habitually move from one place to another. This definition of course does not specify why they move, where they move, how they move, what is the duration of their movement and what they do when they move. So combination of factors individually or collectively with the minimal definition of nomads given earlier, produce a variety of nomadism. Different authors in their respective classifications have emphasized one or more of these factors but without making amply clear why one factor was being considered more important than others.

The repeated shifting of habitat in search of subsistence has been termed as nomadism. This repeated movement is based on realistic considerations having stipulated direction and concentrating themselves around certain centers of operations for obtaining livelihood. Hence "nomadism assumes different forms, depending on climate, topographic conditions, resource availability, the means of livelihood chosen by the wandering group and the preference for settled population. In India there are several types of nomadic groups engaged in a variety of professions like snake charmers, monkey and bear displayers, acrobats, quack surgeons, hunters, food gatherers, artisans, pastoralists and traders (Luiz 161; 204-95). Some of them combine more than one occupation; they may be traders, artisans or trade-pastoralist and so on."[19]

Indian nomads not only add variety and charm but also integrate different aspects of life at different levels. They are one of the factors, which allow the use of the oft-quoted cliché-unity in diversity-in spite of the fact that much has happened in the recent history of India to completely wipe out the autonomy of a sort of numerous small groups of people. Yet the undaunted flame of nomadism must be understood in the wider perspective of Indian civilization.[20] Upliftment of this neglected section of the society is in consonance with the Indian legacy of diverse cultures living together as one.

## NARIKORAVAS, AS MOST BACKWARD CLASS IN TAMIL NADU

Narikoravas do not register prominently in India's complicated caste pecking order. Yet their presence in Tamil Nadu is ubiquitous as an impoverished and vulnerable lot that is on the front line of exposure to economic insecurity and endangered livelihood. They call themselves Vagri, which denotes the native euphemism for spatial and cultural isolation from mainstream population. Moreover, they have been classified as Most Backward Class (MBC) along with other 41 communities in the MBC category and one among the 180 Central lists of Backward Classes notified by the Government of India like Vanniays, Odyar, Kallar etc.[21] As a result they have to compete with them in the very little space that is available. The dominant image of Narikoravas in the minds of many has been one loaded with destitution and shrouded with marginalization. General living condition of Narikoravar community is very low. The entire gamut of socio-economic conditions of Narikoravar community is at low standard and often considered as a menace to people around. Persistent poverty and social taboo conspire to entrap them as modern untouchables.

They have become dregs of society and recyclers of leftovers, which while on the one hand, enable them to survive, and on the other, it forced them into partial settlement habits quietly modifying their nomadic culture.

They have been demanding ST classification since 1990 and their fight for this goes on with verve and vigour. In response to the Tamil Nadu Pazhangudi Vagrivel Workers' Association memorandum submitted to the Government, the State Government has unanimously decided that this community to be included in the S.T list and passed a G.O in favour of Narikoravas, thus giving them the benefits enjoyed by the S.Ts until the Central Government included them in the S.T list. The details of the G.O are given below.[22] The G.O No.666 (Social Welfare Department) dated 29 August 1975, stated that The Government of Tamil Nadu has therefore decided to treat the Narikoravas as backward class and continue to give them all the concessions enjoyed by them hither to as Scheduled Tribe.

In spite of their despicable background, these Narikoravas have not been so far put under the list of Scheduled Tribe in Tamil Nadu, "unlike those in other parts of India like Vagri in UP, Phasephardhi in Maharastra, Hakkipiki in Karnataka, Vagri Igarilok in MP and Naklavandlu in AP and others who come under ST category. The irony is that the government of India has looked upon this community as if they are sophisticated people and thereby classified them under MBC category."[23] Therefore the community feels that it has got a raw deal from successive governments, which often led them to launch agitation against the Government.

Dr.Dipankar Gupta, a sociologist at Jawaharlal Nehru University in New Delhi says that even though the importance of caste hierarchy may have declined, that of caste identity - the voluntary association of people of the same or similar castes- has increased, because as people leave their villages, caste often provides the only ready social network in the big cities.[24] This is more than true in the life of Narikoravas.

Just like their peripatetic way of life, the aspirations of Narikoravas to be included in the list of Scheduled Tribes seems to be going around in circles even though they were given an option to be included in the ST list in 1986 which they coolly rejected. The present Chief Minister of Tamil Nadu, Dr.M. Karunanidhi has promised this people to this effect even though it needs constitutional legislation. In fact "the Centre has reportedly accepted in principle that Narikoravas should be included in the list of STs even as early as 1964, the required formalities are yet to be completed and the matter is still mired in bureaucratic red tape."[25] Hence the question of castes and tribes in India are closely linked to administrative and more so of political considerations.

## NARIKORAVAS, A NEGLECTED LOT

As in other neighboring states, the Tamil Nadu Narikoravas were not able to enjoy the benefits of reservations offered under the SC lists for the past sixty years. Under the Government schemes that benefit the poor, these people are often in the missing list, for example in the distribution of pattas, housing, free gas, TV etc, mainly due to lack of political and economic clout and ultimately left out of the mainstream development process through discrimination. Development strategies adopted in Tamil Nadu, which were populist to the core, have failed to yield the desired result as no remarkable change has occurred in their living conditions.

"The community seemed to be in a transition phase, as the younger generation is least interested in perpetuating the traditional pursuit; rather they want to pursue education to take up regular jobs. For want of support, their wards could not realize their ambition. The pre-requisite for joining school was to have a permanent address and it was what the community hoped to attain nowadays."[26]

## STATEMENT OF THE PROBLEM

There are scores of nomads labelled as gypsies today in Tamil Nadu. But Narikoravas are considered as one the most backward and depressed classes of the society and ill- treated by other classes even in this 21st century. Though socially excluded from mainstream society, Narikoravas continues to be in spotlight in the state and particularly in Vellore district because of their sizeable number and clout. There are no distinct physical traits that identify these people but their dress, language and lifestyle. Their traditional hunting habits have distinguished them as 'Kurvikaran' or birdmen.

Their social and economic status is very low and pathetic even though they look happy and contented with their own lifestyle. If after sixty years of independence, people have to live without proper housing, sanitation, electricity, roads and health, clearly it is not for want of slogans but because of lags in implementation and administrative apathy. The time for delays and half-measures is over to integrate them into the society. Poverty and the absence of development is like a permanent blanket of violence that shrouds this people. The vote bank politics of the present-day society has not moved an inch to make them wriggle out of their vicious circle of poverty. We have squandered a unique opportunity for finding a solution to their endless problems, as they want to be liberated from the shackles of penury through government help and voluntary organizations. Hence it is interesting to study why they are still pegged down to their basic roots in every sphere of living rather than be extricated from the clutches of misery and hopelessness.

Narikoravas labelled as outcasts of the society has been saddled by loss of their unique identity, resource base and plagued by interminable poverty with all its shades and colours. These had cascading effect on this nomadic group directly or indirectly for several decades. Politicians and policy makers offered Nelson's eye to their plight. Time has come for them to be emancipated from the throes of misery as India marches ahead on high growth trajectory, without leaving these people in the lurch.

It has been a long struggle to extract concessions from the Government without being categorized as Scheduled Tribe while remaining as Most Backward Caste, though they are worse than the former. Hence at this juncture, we need to have a closer look at their socio-economic plight that is stoutly reflected in their sources of income and areas of expenditure and rectify the maladies that beset them from time immemorial. Government's creeping efforts to alleviate their plight reinforce the belief that they are still at the periphery of the society.

The status of these people leaves many questions unanswered as offsprings of social exclusion and poverty deprivation. Why these people continue in their plight? Have the development programmes offered any succor to them all these years leaving them permanently trapped in the clutches of poverty? The present study entitled, "An Explorative Study on the Income and Expenditure Pattern of Narikoravas of Vellore District", is an eye- opener in this direction.

## OBJECTIVES

The following are the objectives of the study;

- to trace the origin and settlement details of Narikoravas in Vellore district;
- to find out the income sources of the Narikoravas;
- to examine the expenditure and saving patterns of this nomadic people;
- to identify and analyse the impact of social support schemes on Narikoravas;

- to examine the role of education in their upward mobility; and
- to suggest measures to improve the living conditions of this people.

## HYPOTHESES

1. There is a slow change in the occupation of these people.
2. Education has helped them positively in their upward mobility.
3. Government intervention and involvement of the self- help groups and others have enhanced their income base.

## CONCEPTS USED IN THE STUDY

A sincere attempt was made in this chapter to review the concepts used in the study and previous studies on the subject, as they would be useful for analysis. The main concepts reviewed in this chapter are nomadism, Narikoravas, settlement, migration, poverty, income, expenditure and others.

### Nomadism

Britannica Concise Encyclopedia defines nomadism as a way of life of people who do not live continually in the same place but move cyclically or periodically. It is based on temporary centres whose stability depends on the available food supply and the technology for exploiting it. A hunting and gathering society is a type of nomadic group. Nomadism declined in the 20$^{th}$ century as urban centres expanded and governments sought to regulate or eliminate it. Science Dictionary explains nomadism as a way of life in which a community has no permanent settlement but moves from place to place, usually seasonally and within a defined territory.[27]

### Gypsy

Gypsy is a member of a race of people, originally from North West India. Today, they live in almost every part of the world. Sometime around the tenth century A.D, they embarked on migration that scattered them all over the world.[28] Most of the gypsies speak the language of the people among whom they live. However, many also speak their own language, often called Romany, which belongs to the Indo-Iranian group of languages. The term gypsies are decayed pronunciation of the words "Egyptians" and "Gyptians". One belief is that Indian immigrants from various tribes intermarried and intermixed in Persia forming into a people there, with the name Dom or Rom and that a large number of them then moved into Europe and their descendants are the Romany gypsies of today. They were called Dom meaning, "man" [29].

### Narikoravas

The Tamil Nadu gypsies are nomadic group that once travelled across the Deccan, rearing cattle, hunting, selling herbs and medicinal oils. The English called them gypsies when they arrived in India. They saw these people living in tents (tamboos), roaming from one place to another, like the gypsies of England. Their language is Wagriboli, a mixture of Marathi and Hinudstani.[30]

### Hawking

Hawkers or peddlers or hucksters are "those who try to sell things by going from place to place asking people to buy them."[31] These street vendors are part and parcel of urban life in India. Mostly illegal, their presence is a significant factor in the growing congestion in our urban centres. Tackling their problem is complicated and the issue is highly politicized.

### Settlement

Settlement is a place where people come to live and make their homes, especially where few or no people lived before.

### Social Exclusion

Social exclusion means being unable to access the things in life that most of society takes for granted. The term "social exclusion" probably originated in France where it was used in the 1970's to refer to the flight of those who fell through the net of social protection-disabled people, lone parents and the uninsured unemployed. Rene Lenoir propounded it. The Government's (British) current definition of social exclusion is "social exclusion is a complex and multi- dimensional process. It involves the lack or denial of resources, rights, goods and services and the inability to participate in the normal relationships and activities available to the majority of people, whether in economic, social, cultural or political arenas. It affects both the quality of life of individuals and the equity and cohesion of society as a whole."[32]

'Ruth Levitas develops a model, which identifies three different approaches to the same. The first and the important approach is redistributive discourse (RED), which sees social exclusion as a consequence of poverty. Thus Peter Townsend (1979) argued that poverty should not be understood in terms of subsistence, but in terms of people's ability to participate in the customary life of society. 'Individuals, families and groups can be said to be in poverty when their resources are so seriously below those commanded by the average individual or family that they are, in effect, excluded from ordinary living patterns, customs and activities.'[33]

Another possible definition is "inability to participate effectively in economic, social, political and cultural life, alienation and distance from the mainstream society," (Duffy 1995) or "the dynamic process of being shut out from any of the social, economic, political and cultural systems which determine the social integration of a person in society." (Walker and Walker, 1997)

### Entitlement

Entitlement is a guarantee of access to benefits because of rights, or by agreement through law. It also refers, in a more casual sense to someone's belief that one deserves some particular reward or benefit.[34] Entitlement set includes the full range of resources available to an individual for the realization of his/her potential and include extended entitlements; rights of access to resources which are socially sanctioned, although not legally binding, such as the right of elderly parents to get support from their children.

**Consumption**

Consumption means the act of using goods and services to satisfy current wants. While theoretically there have been practical problems in using consumption, the main problem arises in the treatment of consumer durables.[35]

**Income**

It is the flow of money and goods of an individual or group of individuals of a firm over the same period of time.

**Expenditure**

Expenditure is spending by consumers, investors or the Government. Consumer expenditure is restricted to purchasing real goods and services; acquiring assets or making transfers by individuals is not counted as expenditure. Government expenditure is treated differently.[36]

**Savings**

J.M. Keynes defines savings as the excess of income over expenditure on consumption. He goes on to say that savings as the sum of differences between the money income of individuals and money expenditure on current consumption.[37] "Many researchers have shown that even the poor want to and can save, and that appropriate mechanisms can help realize this potential. Hulme, Moore and Barrientos (2007) are somewhat rueful about the redirection of attention from savings to (micro) credit in recent years, for they perceive this as representing a historic shift in emphasis from thrift as the foundation of finance for the poor in the early twentieth century, to reliance on credit as way out of poverty in the early twenty-first."[38]

**Investment**

Investment means creation of new capital assets like construction of news buildings, new factories and so on. It is an expenditure on capital goods that increases the wealth of the community. But is not an expenditure on consumer goods or a deposit in the bank.[39]

**Borrowings**

Incurring debts to finance spending is known as borrowing. Individuals, firms and Governments do this. Borrowing appears desirable when the benefits from using borrowed money are greater than the interest costs. This may be because of urgent need of individual's spending of sudden falls in income or favourable investment opportunities for firms.[40]

**Poverty**

***Meaning of Poverty***

The state of one who lacks the usual or socially acceptable amount of money or material possession is poverty. Poverty is said to exist when people lack the means to satisfy their basic needs. In this context, the identification of poor people first requires a determination of what constitutes basic needs. They may be defined as narrowly as "those necessary for survival or as broadly as those reflecting the prevailing standard of living in the community."[41]

According to Paul Samuelson and William D.Nordhans, the word "poverty means different things to different people."[42] Clearly, poverty is a condition in which people have inadequate incomes but it is hard to draw an exact line between the poor and the non-poor. Economists have, therefore devised certain techniques, which provide the official definition of poverty.

As a starting point, economists defined poverty as a level of income that is necessary to maintain level of consumption. To double-check this calculation, economists have noted that poor families generally spend one-third of their income on food. Hence the calculations on the cost of subsistence food budget, economists can calculate a minimum subsistence income by multiplying the minimum food budget by a factor of 3. In addition, poverty is a relative term. The notion of a subsistence budget includes subjective questions of taste and social conventions. Housing that is today considered substandard, often includes household appliances and plumbing that were unavailable to the wealthiest citizens of an earlier era.[43]

Hence it may generally be characterized as a state of deprivation, dependence and degradation below physically and socio-culturally acceptable standards.

Poverty is defined on the basis of individuals or societies. Bohwn Rowntree has defined families where "total earnings are insufficient to obtain the minimum necessaries for the maintenance of merely physical efficiency."[44] According to him the biological need is of primary concern. But Holes Bawn has argued, that poverty is always defined according to the conventions of the society in which it occurs. However, it is very common to define poverty as a uni-dimensional poverty. As Wilburn noted for practical purposes, it is easy and convenient to use as indicator like income as certain and to define poverty in terms of specific threshold.[45]

Poverty is situation in which a section of the community is unable to acquire or get even the basic necessities of life such as minimum of food, clothing and shelter. When a substantial section of a society continually lives on a bare subsistence level or below that level, the society is said to be suffering from mass poverty.[46] Mehta and Shah (2001) described poverty as a situation of pronounced deprivation in comparison to well-being.

Andre Beteille (2003) also attempts to relate poverty and inequality. He is of the opinion that in the literature on policy there is a widespread assumption that poverty and inequality are two sides of the same coin. According to him, those who use an absolute concept of poverty find it easier to delink poverty and inequality, particularly when their concern is mainly with inequalities of income and expenditure.

## SCOPE OF THE STUDY

The Narikoravas (gypsies) were traditionally a nomadic tribe and their livelihood depended on hunting. With governmental restrictions on hunting and less hunting opportunities in a rapidly urbanising India, their future is as bleak as ever. According to one of the latest studies on Narikoravas undertaken by M.Sankar, on behalf of Tamil Nadu Pazhangudi Vagrivel Tozhilar Sangam (TAPVATS) in 2008, there are about 29,000 Narikoravas today in Tamil Nadu[47] and they have been one of the most marginalised sections of the society. A majority of these are still leading a nomadic life and remain below the poverty line, with hardly any outside help. Most of their children do not get access to education due to the nomadic life led by their parents. With a ban on hunting animals, they depend mostly on handmade products such as beads, garlands, needles and chains. Many of them continue to live on pavements.

The study will be useful to policy-makers, sociologists, anthropologists, environmentalists, economists, administrators, academicians, social scientists and concerned citizens alike. It will help them to frame a proper perspective planning for developing the centres wherever they stay. Proper planning and Government's own initiatives will help this group to join the mainstream of the Indian society. These people must be shown new vistas of opportunities for their livelihood and income generation. Unless their plight is espoused and brought to the limelight through proper media and conscientization of an awakened citizenry, their destiny will still be trapped in the mire of poverty and misery for many more years to come. Hence this study will be an eye-opener in this direction and eventually bring forth greater advocacy for the eradication of their crippling poverty.

## LIMITATIONS

Though the present study tries to spotlight many problems of the Narikorava community, it is not free from limitations.

Firstly, this study was limited to Vellore district that covered all the 473 families. Thus it was location specific and a micro level study. Therefore, the conclusions can be applied only in similar areas elsewhere.

Secondly, the respondents have furnished their details from their memory. Narikoravas are mostly illiterate lot who did not even keep an account of what they earned and how they spent even on a daily basis unlike the salaried people. Hence eliciting any information regarding their earning and spending habits was a Herculean task. Besides, the study had been restricted to two years only as the problem of recall memory was amply manifested in what they earned and spent.

Thirdly, secondary data related to them were not sufficiently available and many of them were found to be only in Tamil. There was hardly any data related to their income and expenditure pattern in the whole of Tamil Nadu, though in the recent past, some studies related to their socio- economic conditions had been undertaken. However it was a pioneering study undertaken by the researcher on this people in the State and the district in particular.

## CHAPTERIZATION OF THE THESIS

Chapter I covers a general idea of gypsies and Narikoravas in particular. Besides, an overall Study of the district, Statement of the Problem, Objectives, Scope and Limitations of the study are also highlighted.

Chapter II contains the Review of literature, Review of concepts, Terms and Past studies on the subject.

Chapter III deals with Methodology.

Chapter IV describes Socio-Economic profile of the district and Narikoravas.

Chapter V spotlights Socio-Economic aspects of Narikoravas.

Chapter VI illustrates Income and Expenditure Pattern of the Narikoravas.

Chapter VII throws light on the Summary, Conclusions and Policy Implications of the study.

## FOOTNOTES

1. Rudolf, Heredia and Shereen F. Ratnagar., Mobile and Marginalised Peoples, Manohar Publishers and Distributors, New Delhi -2, 2003, p. 21.

2. *ibid.*, p.2.
3. *www.gypsy.com.*
4. L'Osservatore Romano, (English), October 8, 2008, p.18.
5. Mishra P.K. Malhotra K.C., "Nomads in India", Proceedings of National Seminar, Anthropological Survey of India, Kolkota-16, 1982.p.5.
6. "Salesians of Don Bosco Walking with the Gypsies", Salesian Missions Department, Direzione Generale Opere Don Bosco, Roma - 2009, p.12.
7. *ibid.*,p.7.
8. *ibid.*, p. 8.
9. *ibid.*,p.12.
10. *ibid.*, p.8.
11. *www.wikipedia.org/wiki/roma people.*
12. *ibid.*, p.13.
13. 'Nomads', Encyclopedia Britannica, 1964.
14. Mishra, P.K and Malhotra K.C.,(ed.), "Nomads in India", Proceedings of the National Seminar, Anthropological Survey of India, Calcutta- 16, June 1982, p.14.
15. *ibid.*, p.9.
16. Rao, Aparna., Casmir Michael., Nomadism in South Asia, Oxford University Press, New Delhi - 2, 2003, p.10.
17. *ibid.*, p.9.
18. Mishra, P. K, and Malhotra KC., (ed.) "Nomands in India", Proceedings of National Seminar, Anthropological Survey of India, Calcutta - 16,1982,p 12.
19. *ibid.*, p. 9.
20. *ibid*, preface p.VI.
21. Bhatt S.C, and Bhargava Gopal K., (ed.), Land and People of Indian States and Union Territories, Vol,25, Kalpaz Publications, New Delhi-52, 2005,p.4.
22. Deccan Herald, April 19,2006.
    The G.O ordered to treat Narikoravas as backward class but to extend all the concessions enjoyed by S.T by meeting the expenditure in full from the State funds because they were fully convinced that the Narikoravas exhibited all the characteristics of ST tribes. (Report of TN Second Backward Classes Commission, 1985).
23. *www.narikuravarwelfare.org* 31,August 2006.
24. The Economist, 14-20th Feb 2009, p.20.
25. The Hindu, January 14, 2005.
26. *www.narikuravarwelfare.org.*
27. *www.google.com.*
28. *www.findarticles.com.*
29. *www.domresearchcentr.com.*
30. *www.narkoravawelfare.org.*
31. New Oxford Advanced Learner's Dictionary, Oxford University Press, New York, 2006, p. 715.
32. Levitas, Ruth., The Inclusive Society: Social Exclusion and New Labour, Basingstoke, Macmillan,1998.

33. *ibid.*,p.8.
34. *www.wikipedia.com.*
35. Dictionary of Economics, Link Publications, Bharatpur, 2006, p.21.
36. Black, John., A Dictionary of Economics, Oxford University Press, New York, 2005, p.163.
37. Ghodake, N.B., Encyclopedic Dictionary of Economics Vol 5, Mittal Publications, New Delhi, 1966, pp. 640-1.
38. World Economic and Social Survey 2008, Overcoming Economic Insecurity, Academic Foundation, New Delhi - 02, 2009. p.164.
39. *op.cit.*,p.210.
40. Black, John., A Dictionary of Economics, Oxford University Press, New York, 2005, p.36.
41. Samuelson, Paul A.,and William D.Nordhaus, Economics , Mc.Graw-Hill,Inc New York,1995,p.362.
42. *ibid.*,p.363.
43. *ibid.*, p.362.
44. Rowntree, B.S., "Poverty"-A Study of Turn Life , Macmillan London, 1902, p.xvii.
45. Wilbur, G.L., Poverty–A New Perspective, The University Press of Kentucky, Luxington, p.6.
46. Desai, A.R., Rural Sociology in India, Popular Prakasam, 1969,Bombay, p.26-27.
47. Sankar, A., Census of Tamil Vagris, Tamil Nadu Pazhangudi Vagrivel Tozhilar Sangam (TAPVATS), Villupuram, 2008.

# 2

# REVIEW OF LITERATURE

## NOMADS: MEANING

'The term 'nomad' is derived from the Greek word 'nemo' which means to pasture. It refers to people who herd cattle, but with no land of their own and consequently no permanent home. They migrate with all their belongings either on foot or on animals like yaks, asses or mules, ponies or horses, bullocks or buffaloes or camels, either at their will or on their being forced by circumstances, in order to find out better living conditions for themselves. They roam as acrobats or rope dances, magicians, oracles, fortune-tellers, palmist, musicians and dancers, quack physicians or surgeons, veterinarian, peddlers or petty merchants, carriers or artisans. Their way of life has similarity to that of the gypsies, Roma, known all over the world as great wandering communities.'[1]

## THEORIES OF NOMADISM

At present there are two popular groups of theories explaining the origin and essence of the early state of nomadism. The conflict or control theories show the origin of statehood and internal nature in the context of the relations between exploitation, class struggle, war and inter ethnic predominance.[2] The integrative theories were largely oriented to explaining the phenomenon of the state as a higher stage of economic and public integration.

## NOMADIC EMPIRES

The majority of nomadic empires cannot be unambiguously interpreted as either chiefdoms or stated from the viewpoint of either the conflict or integrationist approaches.[3]

In the nomadic empires, the main sign of statehood was absent. According to many current theories of the state, the main distinction between statehood and pre-state forms lies in the fact that chiefdom's ruler has only consensual power i.e., in essence authority, whereas in the state, the government can apply sanctions with the use of legitimated force.

Statehood with its intrinsic bureaucracy appears fairly late in the epoch of post-Alexandrian Hellenistic states and in the Roman Empire. However, what term should be used to describe the politics of nomads? "Considering their non-state features, I prefer to characterize the nomadic politics as "super complex chiefdoms."[4] The nomadic empires, as super complex chiefdoms, provide a real prototype of a particular kind of early state. The fundamental difference between the nomadic empires was that their "centers" were highly developed only in the military aspect while they were less developed than the exploited or conquered territories in socio-economic complexity and other attributes of civilizations. They were actual 'peripheries' in themselves. In this case, the nomadic empire can be defined as nomadic society organized on the military-hierarchical principle, occupying a quite large space and exploiting the nearby territories, as rule, by external forms of exploitation, robbery, war and indemnity, extortion of "presents" non-equivalent trade and tribute.

According to Barfield, nomadic empires were organized in the form of "imperial confederations". The confederations had an autocratic and state like look from outside. They were created to bring the surplus products of agrarian peasants to the steppe nomads. Their inner structure was consultative and tribal in form.[5]

## NOMADIC CIVILIZATION

Sorokin, Toynbee and others have followed comparative civilization approach. In 1934 Toynbee suggested that pastoral nomads could constitute a special form of solidified civilization. It is beyond question that pastoral nomadism is special world that stands in opposition to the world of agrarian civilizations. But nomadic civilization is a metaphor rather than a scientific definition. Hence he suggests that all types of human cultures could be characterized as civilizations because each civilization is based on a particular psycho-cultural unity and goes through the stages of growth, prosperity and collapse. Its prosperity occurred during the very long period from the First Millennium to the middle of the Second millennium. During this period a number of settled agricultural civilizations appeared and collapsed. The same fate was met for a many nomadic societies during the period of nomadic steppe empires. It is not likely that the nomads thought of themselves as unified cultural group standing in opposition to other nations and civilizations.[6]

The nomadic societies were doomed to remain peripheral because the core often exploited semi peripheral, whereas the nomadic empires were never exploited by agrarian civilizations. The mobile mode of the pastoral nomads did not provide the opportunity to make great accumulations and their society was based on the gift economy. The rulers of the steppe empires between the tribal chiefs and stockbreeders distributed all plunder.

Barfield established the synchrony between the growth and decline of the nomadic empires and similar process in China. In the emerging Europe-centered capitalist world system, the nomads were allotted quite another position. Machine, technology, firearms and new sources of energy changed the balance of power to their disadvantage. Since that time, the steppe hinterland has ceased to play an important role in the dynamics of world-system processes.

To sum up, it could be stated that nomadic empire was a distinctive democratic form of mode of production. Inside, it was a super complex chiefdom. It was based on the redistribution of profits from war, extortion, and international trade by the khan (chief). On the outside, it was a militaristic collective exploiter of agrarian states and civilizations. The problem of nomads and the outside world was so complex and many-sided that there seemed to be no way in which it could be simplified. Each nomadic society must be reassessed when applied to another nomadic society. That which is true of nomads today may not apply to the nomads of ancient time or the Middle Ages.

## THEIR LINKAGE

It is pertinent to know that nomadic way of life did not evolve in a vacuum. Most of the communities today have deep historical roots. For instance the origins of Killekytha or the leather - picture exhibitors can be traced back to as early as 1520.The Rabaris or the pastoral nomads of Rajasthan are referred to by Abul Faizl in the Ain–e-Akbari as being paid in grain and cash for their services as mounted couriers throughout the Mughal period. Some of the agro- pastoral communities like the Abhiras find mention in the Mahabharatha as robbers and highwaymen. The itinerant Gaduliya Lohars or blacksmiths spoke of how "kalka devi" cursed them to a nomadic way of life. They also refer to Chittorgarh in Rajasthan as their ancestral home, which they left, fell into the hands of Mughal Army in 1568.[7]

## DIVERSE GROUPS

The sheer diversity of the livelihoods of each of these nomadic communities makes it a compelling reading. Each one occupied a particular socio-economic niche, fulfilling a specific need of village or sedentary communities. There were the Ghatiya Jogis or makers of grinding tones for household use, the Nadiwallahs who were welcomed by farmers for the manure their cattle provided to the fields, the Hakkipikkis of Southern India who made a living from hunting or selling wild animals or the Vaidus or traditional healers who made medicines from forest plants. Sociological studies showed that 3 to 20 such communities of forgers, healers, entertainers or specialized service providers like the Lohars or the blacksmiths visited villages. However, each of these livelihoods was threatened due to a multiplicity of factors, be it factory made goods, modern means of entertainment or strict wildlife laws.

For instance, when there were no roads or trucks or big markets, it was the Banjaras who made the mobile meat transporters. They would herd cattle in large numbers from Rajasthan to Uttar Pradesh, to slaughterhouses. Banjara women like Santara, would buy goods in bulk and then do door-to-door selling in villages. Santara's job, though decades old, was much like that of the modern day saleswoman.

The Bhopas earn a living by reciting tales from the canvas piece. Some of the tales of the Bhopas carry on through the night. According to them, today, no one is interested in listening to their stories anymore as people have switched on to radio and TV.

The Gadoliya Lohars, got their name from the gaddi or carts used to move from place to place. Today people prefer to buy steel and aluminum goods from the market rather than use the rickety tools that are crafted by the blacksmiths or the Lohars. Lohars therefore find themselves constantly on the move searching for new markets.

According to Bacon, different forms of nomadism have been classified as true nomads, semi-nomads and semi-sedentary, depending on the nature of movement. Nomadic tribes have always been a source of suspicion to the sedentary people.[8]

"It was the colonial period which brought about significant changes for the nomads. In the colonial period, the British normalized a set of notions about such groups that echoed European ideas about the gypsies. They listed such groups that posed a 'threat' to settled society and introduced a legislative measure, the Criminal Tribes Act (CTA) in 1871 and as a result nearly 200 such communities stood 'notified' as criminal. From the very beginning, the British regarded mobility as 'backward' and nomads as uncontrollable and hence potentially criminal. Furthermore, new forest regulations after the 1860s deprived numerous pastoralists of grazing land and most foragers lost free access to forests. The construction of canals, roads and the laying of railway lines led to complete disruption of migration patterns of many nomadic groups during the 19th century. [7]

It was the colonial revenue policies which destroyed the itinerant communities' earlier trading practices."[9] "In Europe, nomadism had come to be equated with vagrancy and poverty; criminalization of the poor led to the idea of 'dangerous classes.' Transferred to South Asia, these concepts paired increasingly well with those concerned with recently discovered caste system, within which each entity was conceived of as fixed, with clearly definable features.[10] Nomadism, per se is not a criterion for low-caste status. All nomads are not low-ranking castes.

## CLASSIFICATION OF NOMADS

Nomads may be classified as pastoralists, foragers and peripatetics.

### Pastoralists or Animal Husbanders

This community is primarily dependent on livestock. Their degree of dependence may vary seasonally and even annually. Included in this category are those known as agro-pastoralists and migratory peasant graziers. Pastoralists raise herds and move with them so as not to deplete pasture beyond recovery in any one area.

Pastoral nomadism may be defined as distinct form of food-producing economy in which extensive mobile pastoralism is the predominant activity and in which majority of the population is drawn into periodic pastoral migrations. It is a single form of food-producing economy, which remains different from other food-extracting economies (for example, from different forms of hunting, fishing and gathering) and from other food-producing economies (eg. different forms of slash and burn and shifting horticulture and plough agriculture) even in a supplementary capacity.

Pastoral nomadism in its pure manifestations is characterized by absence of agriculture. Pure nomads are only recorded in certain regions of pastoral nomadism (North Eurasia, High Inner Asia, the European steppes, Arabia, the

Sahara), but even in these regions pastoral nomadism co-exists as a rule with other forms of pastoralism. Semi-nomadic pastoralism is much more widespread throughout the world.[11] It is linked to other food-producing economies by a series of transitional forms at the basis of which lies the gradually diminishing specific position of pastoralism.[12]

"Freguson and Adam Smith were claiming that the development of pastoralism led to social differentiation. Kant saw the origins of statehood in the conflict between nomads and agriculturists."[13] Nomads and pastoralists (no precise differentiation was made between the two) were looked upon not so much as a particular ethnographical phenomenon, but as a factor in the general development of mankind.

**Hunter-gatherers or Foragers**

Their principal economic strategy consists of hunting (including fishing) and gathering/collecting, as they do not have any regular access to cultivable land. Since the foods foraged are patchily distributed, mobility of varying degrees is required. Nomadic hunter-gatherers have by far the longest-lived subsistence method in human history, following seasonally available wild plants and game.

**Peripatetics**

They are mostly non-food producing extracting, preferentially endogamous, itinerant community subsisting over long periods mainly on the scale of goods and more on nomadic clients; some may have a little land, houses or herds and might even forage a little. Depending on the nature of goods and or services offered and the density of the relevant clientele, the degree of mobility varies. Other terms used in recent years to describe peripatetics are 'symbiotic nomads', 'service nomads', 'non-food-producing nomads' and 'trade nomads.'[14] Peripatetic nomads are more common in industralised nations, traveling from one territory to another and offering a trade wherever they go. But the group in question may be called as foragers ie., those mainly endogamous groups whose principal economic and traditional subsistence strategy consists of gathering/collecting/and hunting (using various methods and including fishing) and who have little or no regular access to cultivable land. Since the foods collected or hunted are patchily and seasonally distributed, mobility to varying degrees is a must. Hence a multi-resource approach to nomadism enables us to better grasp the realities of economic practice and changing group identity.[15]

As per their lifestyle, there are complex reasons why people follow such a tradition. Being on the move, nomads are able to tap into wider markets for the services they provide. It seems to represent a shrewd economic strategy-one of optimizing benefits and minimizing risks by being constantly on the move. Yet the reaction of most policy makers and development agencies has been to view nomadic groups as being 'under-developed' and in need of integration with the rest of the Indian society.

From the observations of the different professions or economic groups among the nomads, two common elements emerge. First, each group is affected by modernization and it is in increasing conflict with sedentary villagers with whom they no longer seemed to share symbiotic relation. Secondly, as a result of changing times, the value of their occupation has gone down. Increasingly, these nomadic people are turning to labour markets or construction sites for jobs.

## THE NOMADS OF TAMIL NADU

"In Tamil Nadu, various folk groups who belong to different ethnic communities have led a nomadic or semi nomadic life and in economic limbo from generation to generation without having any piece of land, permanent settlements, or other material goods which are considered essential for a civilized and comfortable living. Most of the nomads have made a living as singers and dancers (*Boom-Boom Maattukkaarar, Narikuravas* or *Vagri*), puppeteers (*Marathi Rao* or *Mandigar*) acrobats and tight rope walkers (*Doms* or *Dombar*), monkey and snake charmers (*Kaattu Naaikans*), whip dancers, (*Chaattaiyadikkaara Naaikan*), fortune-tellers, magicians or conjurers (*Kanikkan, Kambalathu Naaikan and Malaipandaaram*), record dancers (*Kaatu*

*Valluvan*), craft and doll-makers (potters migrated from Rajasthan), lead-coaters (*Panikkan* and *Naaikan*), tattooing artists, stone-cutters, and basket makers (*Kuravas* and *Malaikuravas*). Among these nomadic communities, *Boom-Boom Maattukkaaran* or *Poövidaiyan* (means flower neat herds) community is prominent in northern Tamil Nadu with thousands of people who are skilled in their respective folk performing arts."[16]

## ORIGIN OF NARIKORAVAS

There is a general agreement that the gypsies originated in India and moved to various places of the world. "In fact their history, accumulated through the medium of their spoken language can be traced back to India, where in all probability they originated."[17]

"The gypsies may be defined as an ethnic minority with a number of inherited physical features and distinctive language related to Sanskrit. They are believed to have their origin in north-west India and have resided in Europe since the middle age,"[18] known by different names such as Roma, Sinti, Manouches, Kale, Gitans, Yeniches and others. Worldwide there are an estimated 8 to 10 million Roma.[19]

"Often plagued by persecution, exile, inhospitality, rejection, suffering and discrimination, gypsy history is shaped by permanent wandering that distinguishes them from others. This has given rise to an identity with its own languages and a culture and religiosity with their own traditions and a strong sense of belonging, with its relevant bonds. So with them humanity is enriched by a real cultural heritage."[20] Indeed their life was a saga of resilience in the midst of penury and their wisdom was not written down in books, but that did not make it any less eloquent.

According to a popular tale, it was believed that they have originated from Aravalli hills, Mevar and Gujarath and landed in Tamil Nadu escaping from the persecution and conversion drive of the Muslim rulers between the sixth and seventh century. Besides during the reign of Sivaji, these people seemed to have escaped the Muslim subjugation.

## THE SIBS AND RITUALS

Among the Narikoravas, all the members tracing descent through the same ancestor most often did not form a local group. In other words, the decent group seldom coincided with the local group. As a result, the two aspects of descent and residence remain distinct through related aspects, and these have been dealt with in the same manner. The first aspect, of descent and consequently the descent groups is, here, dealt with first.[21]

## THE SIBS

The Narikoravas trace their descent patrilineally and are divided into two exogamous halves-the Bekho-maron-valo and the Bokdo- maron-valo. Each of these halves therefore constitutes a patrimoiety. The two patrimoieties derive their name from the nature of sacrifices they make to their respective deities whom they call them as devi (goddess). The members of the Bekho-maron-valo moiety sacrifice he-buffaloes or Bekho to their goddess and the name of this moiety translated into English would be 'buffalo-sacrificing-people'. On the other hand, the name Bokdo-maron-valo translated into English would be 'Goat-Sacrificing-People' as the members of this moiety sacrifice he-goats or bokdo to their goddess.

Each of the patrimoieties has further sub-divisions. The members of each of these sub-divisions trace descent from a common mythical ancestor and are scattered over a large area. No such sub-division has all its members in one place, in other words the sub-divisions are not co-residential. It would therefore be appropriate to call each of these sub-divisions a sib. The sibs belonging to the Bekho-maron-valo moiety are the Gujratho and the Paawar and those sibs belonging to the Bokdo-maron-valo are the Mewada, the Dabhi and the Selyo.

All the members of a sib are believed to have descended from a single ancestor, the Guru of the sib, who is assigned a divine origin from the devi of the sib. From this Guru had descended all other ancestors who had founded the various sub-divisions of the sib. The sibs thus seem to have undergone 'drift segmentation' giving rise to a 'merging segmentary series' of sub-sibs.[22]

The extent of segmentation however varies from one sib to the other. All the sibs and their sub divisions are referred to by the Narikoravas generally as Jath. They have assigned the sub-sibs relative positions on a scale of seniority, based on the seniority of the founding Guru. The division of the sibs and the scale of seniority of the sub-sibs have ritual significance but no significance in marriage. All the sibs belonging to the Bekho-maron-valo moiety have marital exchange relationship with all the sibs belonging to the Bokdo-maron-valo moiety and do not have any such relationship among them, as each moiety is exogamous.

The sibs belonging to the Bekho-maron-valo moiety, the Gujratho and the Paawar, have undergone considerable segmentation, more so the Gujratho. All the members of the Gujratho sib are believed to be descendents of their Guru Basingdeo whose mother was the sib devi-Vairagan. The descendents of this Guru were the eponymic Gurus of the sub-sibs the Jamlo, the Sakuru and the Govindo in the order of decreasing seniority. Of these three sub-sibs, only the Jamlo sub-sib has further sub-divisions. There are four sub-sibs under the Jamlo sub-sib - the Nan Singh, the Then Singh, the Kal Singh, and Singhdi, founded by their eponymic gurus and presented here in the order of their seniority.[23]

The rest of the members are said to be descendants of the first two large groups ie., Dabi and Selio from Mevado and Jogan from Gujarato ancestors.

## ARE NARIKORAVAS PRODUCTS OF CULTURAL DRAG OR LAG?

Cultural lag is one of the theories often used to describe the factors that influence cultural changes. Ogburn first described the theory of cultural lag in 1915. He defines cultural lag as a "lag that occurs when one of two parts of culture which are correlated changes before or in greater degree than the other part does, thereby causing less adjustment between the two parts that existed previously."(Ogburn 1957)

When he described socio-cultural change and culture in terms of "parts" he relied on a very common model of the day that compared society and culture to an organic model in which the various "parts" were analogous to the organs of the human body. He draws an analogy of the cars that run off the road on curves. He believed that the answer lay in the culture of road building.

According to him, four critical factors drive cultural change. They are invention, accumulation, diffusion and adjustment. (Ogburn, 1950) He uses India at the time of Buddha as an example of a lag in which religion was the primary motivating force behind a great deal of social change. (Ogburn 1957)

To distinguish between different types of lag, Brinkman prefers to term socio-cultural lag, rather than merely cultural lag. He uses this term "socio-cultural lag" which he attributes to indicate that lags involve both social as well as cultural elements.[24]

Historically, the resolution of a cultural lag has been a positive outcome. But it is not clear whether the resolution of a drag will be positive. Cultural drag may have a significant negative effect on society at least in the short term. A simple way of viewing the difference between a cultural lag and drag can be seen in the motivating factors that underline the cultural changes that occur. In a lag, society is being coaxed or pulled, more or less willingly in a given direction by a perceived benefit. Conversely, in cultural drag, the motivation becomes more of a push. This motivating force is often an unpalatable choice of the lesser of two evils. When choices are unpalatable, individuals and societies are more reluctant to make changes and tend to resist the push. This divergence is the root of many social conflicts. This can be seen in the modern problem of resource depletion.

Cultural drag is not part of the material but rather the non-material part of culture. It is the result of laws that have not been updated to reflect changing social patterns and needs.

The sociological study and empirical testing of cultural lag and cultural drag, as they relate to individual's perceived benefit, may improve individual decision-making by providing the individual with information they may not otherwise have. This could make these decisions more beneficial for both the individual and the society.

## THE THEORY OF SOCIAL EXCLUSION

The basic concerns of Narikoravas cannot be understood as an independent factor without knowing the wide range of issues involved in it. Hence the basis of their penury and morbidity cannot be understood as single factor that retards them all through their life, based on limited theoretical underpinning. Rather it must be understood within the ambit of exclusion that manifests itself in varied forms.

The term 'social exclusion' is a relatively recent origin, coined in France by Rene Lenoir in 1974 who has focused this concept in the context of poverty and deprivation found in the French society, of people who are handicapped, aged, invalids, abused children, asocial persons and other social 'misfits' who come under the banner of employment, sociability, citizenship, democratic participation etc.[25] But it is be pointed out that Georg Simmel, a German sociologist outlined a sociological perspective on social exclusion and inclusion as early as 1908 that may even be superior to current discourse on social exclusion.[26]

"It is a fundamental and wide category that may include in its arch, the notions of poverty, hunger, unemployment and destitution. It is about all those individuals or groups that are excluded from the basic means of livelihood, but it is also about those excluded from the process of political and economic decision-making, and those excluded from any conceptualization of social security. At a wider level, it may refer to exclusion from education, health care and ultimately the freedom that an individual must have to organise or control his or her life in a given social setting."[27]

The notion of social exclusion, may serve as a criterion to assess alternative approaches or systems of economic development or social progress, for each such system or approach would typically generate diverse, though overlapping, groups that may be regarded as the beneficiaries. By implication they would be excluded from the fruits of progress. In his criterion of assessment of alternative social states Rawls (1971) focuses solely on the well-being of the worst-off individuals. We are concerned with the condition of all those excluded from the basic means of livelihood or what Rawls has called "primary social goods". These are the things that every rational man is presumed to want, including rights and liberties, opportunities and powers, income and wealth and the bases of self-respect. These are also goods that enhance the capabilities and freedoms of human beings to do the things that they want and pursue the goals that they desire. To exclude individuals from these goods would imply a denial of certain basics that are legitimately the due of every human being.[28]

## Understanding Poverty as a New Paradigm Shift

### *Multidimensional Poverty*

Since the late 1980's the term 'poverty' has been gradually substituted by the term 'exclusion' in the political discourse of several European countries. Prompted by debates in Europe on new forms of poverty in the wake of crisis of the welfare state, development studies started focusing on the notion of social exclusion (Arjan de Haan 2004). A number of early studies of social exclusion claim that poverty and social exclusion differ in two fundamental things. Poverty, considered, as an income deprivation is one-dimensional, whereas, social exclusion is related to a broad range of aspects of deprivation and hence it is multi-dimensional (Bergham, 1995). The concept of social exclusion's multi-dimensionality also allowed it to become the site for different and competing constructions of the policy problems and its solution (Louise Humpage, 2006).

Social exclusion must be placed in the broad context of capability deprivation since characterisation of poverty as a simply shortage of income is an ancient thinking and properly defined has enormous influence on the kind of lives we can lead. The impoverishment of our lives is the result of frequent inadequacy of income and in this sense, low income must be an important cause of poor living. Ultimately poverty must be seen in terms of poor living, rather than just as lowness of incomes. Income may be the most prominent means for a good life without deprivation, but it is not the influence on the lives we can lead. We must look at impoverished lives, and not just at depleted wallets.

The idea of seeing poverty as a multidimensional factor was seen even from the days of Aristotle. He linked the richness of human life to the necessity to "first ascertain the function of man" followed by exploring 'life in the sense of activity'. According to him an impoverished life is one without the freedom to undertake important activities that a person has reason to choose."[29]

Poverty of living received systematic attention also in the early empirical works on the quality of life by such thinkers like William Petty, George King, Francois Quesnay, Antoine Lavoisier, Joseph Louis Lagrange and others. Adam Smith was impelled to define "necessaries" in terms of their effects on the freedom to live non- impoverished lives (such as the 'ability to appear in public without shame'). Hence the view of poverty as capability deprivation ie., poverty seen as the lack of capability to live minimally decent life) has a far-reaching analytical history. "No concept of poverty can be satisfactory if it does not take adequate note of the disadvantages that arise from being excluded from shared opportunities enjoyed by others."[30]

In India, there are several structural factors, which are responsible for poverty. Therefore instead of looking at poverty as a cause of exclusion, one has to find the root cause of poverty. In doing so, they can also link poverty with other indicators of exclusion.

The reason is, though poverty is one of the many causes of exclusion, the reverse is also happening in a sense that exclusion causes poverty and deprivation that we find interminably among semi-nomads like the Narikoravas whose poverty is not the only determinant or indicator of exclusion.

*Social Exclusion and Capability Deprivation*

The capability perspective on poverty is inescapably multidimensional since there are distinct capabilities and functioning that one has reason to value. One has good reason to value not being excluded from social relations, and in this sense, social exclusion may be directly a part of capability poverty. In fact Adam Smith's focus on deprivation a not 'being able to appear in public without shame' is a good example of a capability deprivation that takes the form of social exclusion. This is linked to the importance of taking part in the life of the community which means that the individual lives an inescapably "social life". Smith's general point that the inability to interact freely with others is an important derivation in itself (like being undernourished or homeless) and has the implication that some types of social exclusion must be seen as constitutive components of the idea of poverty - indeed must be counted among its core components.

Secondly, being excluded from social relations can lead to other deprivations as well, thereby further limiting our living opportunities. For example, being excluded from the opportunity to be employed or to receive credit may lead to economic impoverishment that may, in turn, lead to other deprivations such as undernourishment or homelessness.

Social exclusion can, thus be constitutively a part of capability deprivation as well as instrumentally a cause of diverse capability failures. The case for seeing social exclusion as an approach to poverty is easy enough to establish within the general perspective of poverty as capability failure. He investigated the characteristics of social exclusion within a broader concept of deprivation in the form of inability to do things that one has reason to want to do,[31] even for meeting the necessaries for leading a decent life like shoes. "The poorest person of either sex would be ashamed to appear in public without them." Hence social exclusion must be placed within the broader perspective of poverty as capability deprivation rather than merely as lowness of income, which is the standard criterion of identification of poverty. "Besides, deprivation in various spheres of social life has to be seen as one of the vital area to be considered in relation to poverty."[32] Hence

- "Poverty can be sensibly identified in terms of capability deprivation; the approach concentrates on deprivations that are intrinsically important;
- There are influences on capability deprivation -and thus on real poverty-other than lowness of income (income is not the only instrument in generating capabilities).
- The instrumental relation between low income and low capability is variable between different communities and different individuals (the impact of income on capabilities is contingent and conditional).[33]

The last issue is particularly important in considering and evaluating public action aimed at reducing inequality or poverty.

First, the relationship between income capability would be strongly affected by the age of the person, by gender and social roles, by location and other variations over which a person may have no or only limited control.

Secondly, there are some "coupling" of disadvantages between income deprivation and adversity in converting income into functionings. eg. handicaps such as age or disability or illness reduce one's ability to earn an income.

Thirdly, distribution within the family raises further complications with the income approach to poverty.

Fourthly, relative deprivation in terms of incomes can yield absolute deprivation in terms of capabilities. Being relatively poor in a rich country can be a great capability handicap, even when one's absolute income is high in terms of world standards.

The capability perspective of poverty is to enhance the understanding of the nature and causes of poverty and deprivation by shifting primary attention away from means (viz., income) to ends that people have reason to pursue, and, correspondingly, to the freedom to satisfy these ends.

Hence based on the capability approach, Dr. A.K. Sen in his latest book "The Idea of Justice" says, 'poverty will be much more intense than what can be deduced from the income data" due to the variations in the distribution of wealth within the family. For instance, if the family's income is used disproportionately to advance the interests of only certain individuals, then the aggregate family income may not adequately reflect the deprivation of neglected members like physically challenged or the aged.

The link between resources and poverty is rather complex. "It is variable and deeply contingent on the characteristics of the respective people and the environment in which they live, both natural and social. Income is not an indicator of one's standard of living, the kinds of lifestyles that people can lead depend on many factors, including diversities in the physical environment, variations in social climate, differences in relational perspectives as mentioned earlier. So different kinds of disadvantages related to capability deprivation can be a critically important consideration in understanding poverty and in preparing public policy to tackle poverty.'[34] Therefore the way most governments measure poverty by basing it on income, may be flawed perception of well-being.[35] Putting in place the right institutions and entitlements is a step towards a more just society.

**Studies on Social Exclusion**

Since the concept of social exclusion has grown out of the European discourses, the term is perceived differently over the years. "The interpretation of social exclusion like the research in France by Pauganm (1995) emphasizes income deprivation as a part of social exclusion. But the Anglo-Saxon tradition continues to define the two as separate. This is for example illustrated in the common question whether social exclusion is responsible for cause of poverty." (Arjan de Haan and Pelay, 2004)[36] Here the researcher inclines to the former one that income deprivation is part of social exclusion, rather than the latter one that treats them separate.

Skires (1995) has propounded social exclusion on three categories viz.,

- Solidarity paradigm considers exclusion as rapture of social bond between the individual and the society.
- Specialization paradigm which considers exclusion equivalent to discrimination which denies individuals full access to participation in exchange or interaction, and
- Monopoly paradigm which views social order as coercively imposed through hierarchical power relations.

Each of these paradigms can be filled into the analysis in one-way or another. Most of the analysis and conception of exclusion follow one of these paradigms.

Prof. Throat has defined social exclusion as the denial of equal opportunities imposed by certain groups of society upon others, which leads to inability of an individual to participate in the basic political, economic and social functioning of the society.

Amartya Sen too considers various meanings and implications of social exclusion. He considers four major ways in which this exclusion could occur. They are:

- Direct exclusion or unfavourable exclusion i.e. violating fair norms of exclusion
- Unfavourable inclusion i.e., violating fair norms of inclusions
- Active exclusion i.e., exclusion through direct government polices
- Passive exclusion i.e., the exclusion unintentionally happening because of various circumstances and factors.[37]

**Active and Passive Exclusion**

A potentially useful distinction is between active and passive exclusion. When for example immigrants or refugees are not given political status, it is an active exclusion and this applies to many of the deprivations from which minority communities suffer in Europe and Asia like nomads of India. However when the deprivation comes about through social processes in which there is no deliberate attempt to exclude, the exclusion can be seen as a passive kind. Poverty and isolation generated by a sluggish economy may be an example in question.

Relational exclusion may be brought about by a deliberate policy to exclude some people from some opportunities. For example, the decision of the U.S Congress a couple of years ago to exclude permanent residents who are not US citizens from certain types of federal benefits.

A sizeable segment of the population is excluded from translating their unfulfilled needs into effective demand in the food market because of lack of purchasing power. This predicament is the result of a variety of economic disadvantages, some of which can be more directly linked to relational perspective of exclusion than others. The incidence of undernourishment is much greater in India than in sub-Saharan Africa. The proportion of undernourished children in India is a gigantic 40 to 60 per cent (Scrimshaw, 1998, Svedberg, 1998) despite there being no "food shortage" that leads to deprivation - in this case, to a sharp fall in the purchasing power of the affected population.[38]

Sometimes an active exclusion can bring about other exclusionary consequences that are not part of the plan of exclusion but nevertheless are the results of the directly aimed exclusion even though they may not have been clearly anticipated. Thus the real relevance of an exclusionary perspective is thus conditional on the nature of the process.

Thus, there is an agreement that has emerged among various scholars like Room (1995), Atkinson (1998) and A. K. Sen (2000) about the attributes of social exclusion.

**The Language of Exclusion**

Social exclusion can indeed arise in a variety of ways. However there may be a temptation to dress up every deprivation as a case of social exclusion. For example, hunger and starvation relate to entitlement failure that can result from a variety of causes like

- Hunger caused by a crop failure that makes a peasant family lose its traditional food supply
- Hunger resulting from unemployment through the loss of purchasing power.
- Hunger induced by a fall in real wages as result of relative price changes.
- Hunger precipitated by the removal of food subsidies to a particular group on which that group may stoutly rely.

While each of these developments can be described in the language of exclusion, for example (1) being excluded from enjoying a normal crop (2) being excluded from employment (3) exclusion from food market because of low purchasing power (4) exclusion from food subsidy arrangements, there are other quite different casual patterns, some of which are more fruitfully described in the language of exclusion.[39] Not using credit market need not be seen as intrinsically distasteful as one may follow the advice of Polonius, "Neither a borrower, nor a lender be". But not to have access to the credit market can, through causal linkages lead to other deprivations, such as income poverty or take up initiatives to further ones income. These kinds of exclusions can have instrumental importance though they may not be impoverishing in themselves but they can lead to impoverishment of human life through their casual consequences. Landlessness is similarly an instrumental exclusion as a family in a peasant society like India may be deeply handicapped to be without land may seem like being without a limb of one's own.

Besides, relational deprivations may, easily enough have both constitutive and instrumental importance. For example not to be able to mix with others may directly impoverish a person's life and additionally reduce economic opportunities that come from social contact.[40]

**Diversity of Exclusions**

*Inequality and Relational Poverty:* This kind of poverty relates to new styles of consumption that may get established in a poor country as a result of the influence or imitation of consumption levels in richer countries with the onset of globalisation.

*Labour Market Exclusions:* The rejection of the freedom to participate in the labour market is one of the ways of keeping people in bondage and captivity, while the freedom to enter markets promote economic growth and industrialisation. The freedom to participate in labour markets has a basic role in social living and can have both constitutive relevance and instrumental importance. Prof.Throat points out that the Action Aid's all India study reveals the discrimination in labour markets operates through exclusion in hiring and wage allocation. The study shows that in 36 per cent of the villages, the SCs face discrimination in terms of wage payments. Moreover, in about one-third of the villages the SCs were excluded from employment in construction of houses.[41]

*Credit Market Exclusions:* Traditionally we have observed that the poor have not been welcomed to the banking fold by the banks and financial institutions with a misconception that they are not bankable and there is no business opportunity in offering services to the under-privileged and poor particularly in rural areas under several obvious pretext. Given the belief that Credit is Human Right as advocated by Nobel Laureate Professor Muhammad Yunus, the poor can overcome poverty by generating their own employment and income. Access to affordable financial services, especially credit enlarges livelihood opportunities and empowers the poor to take charge of their lives. Hence financial inclusion is a sine quo non factor for inclusive growth.[42]

*Gender related Exclusions and Inequality:* Persistence of gender inequality is more pronounced in India and other developing economies. The neglect of the interests of women relates closely to their being excluded from employment opportunities, basic education, and landownership. It has been found in international comparisons and also in intergenerational comparisons within a large country like India that women's schooling and women's employment opportunities have profoundly powerful effects in reducing not only gender bias mortality, but also in curtailing fertility.

*Health Care:* This is an extensive problem in many Asian countries.

*Food Market and Poverty:* This is a rampant phenomenon that we witness today in India as poor are not able to sustain their livelihood with purchases made from the cheapest food markets.

**Persistent Unemployment and Exclusion**

There are other effects other than loss of income associated with unemployment. Unemployment is a major cause of social exclusion that may cause a person to be subjected to unequal inclusion in an exploitative occupation. European concepts usually consider deprivation that begins with the loss of employment, which in turn leads to a significant degradation in living standards, that is, increased risk of poverty, leading to its ill-effects that one encounters in social activities. We consider latter relationship more important as it creates a spiral of insecurity and inequality, which will further pitchfork poverty with all it ramifications.

Some of these effects can be helpful in analysing the idea of social exclusion.

- *Loss of Current Output:* Unemployment involves wasting of productive power since a part of potential output is not realized through unemployment.
- *Skill Loss and Long Run Damage:* People not only learn by doing, they also unlearn by not doing, that is, by being out of work and out of practice
- Loss of freedom and social exclusion
- Psychological harm and misery
- Ill-health and mortality
- Loss of human relations
- Motivational loss and future work

- Gender and racial inequality
- Weakening of social values

Thus poverty and unemployment may be deemed to be the most significant and fundamental categories of social exclusion. The perspective of social exclusion reinforces rather than competes the understanding of poverty as capability deprivation.

Exclusion is one route to capability failure and poverty what may be called "unfavourable inclusion" or unfavourable exclusion. Once social exclusion is seen within the broader concept of capability deprivation, there is no difficulty in seeing the diverse origins of the failure to have adequate basic capabilities.[43] And these deprivations will have diverse origins and may take disparate forms as seen earlier. At the same time one can also observe that such discrimination and denials are not peculiar in terms of caste, but certain other excluded groups such as transgender, HIV affected, disabled, nomads etc who also experience exclusion in one form or another.

The absence of "social safety nets" when economic growth falters and lives are battered, probably afflicts people of Asia and Africa much more than western Europe that insulates itself with features of welfare state.[44]

**Social Exclusion and Human Rights**

The notion of exclusion may also be widened to incorporate the notion of rights. For example, one may examine the notion of exclusion from the right to free speech, religion or in the case of the young, the right to have secure childhood. Exclusion from these rights constitutes a fundamental violation of individual liberty.

Sixty years ago, the Universal Declaration of Human Rights declared, "Everyone has the right to standard of living adequate for the health and well-being of himself and of his family, including food, clothing, housing and medical care and necessary social services, and the right to security in the event of unemployment, sickness, disability, widowhood, old age or other lack of livelihood in circumstances beyond his control."[45]

In trying to gauge the possible damage from these sources of insecurity, "economists have distinguished between idiosyncratic risks, generated by individual and isolated events such as illness, accident or a crime and covariant risks, which are attached to events that hit a large number of people simultaneously, such as an economic shock or climatic hazard, and often involve multiple and compounding costs."[46]

Hence "it is primarily the responsibility of Governments to address these threats by removing underlying vulnerabilities, greatly reducing the exposure of households and communities and supporting their recovery to find their footing in the society. This is particularly vital in societies with an increasingly complex division of labour, where high levels of trust, long-term investments in physical, human and social capital that are key ingredients of long term prosperity and stability. In this respect, providing economic security is complementary component of any virtuous circle involving creative markets and inclusive political structures."[47]

In this context, child labour, which is so rampant among the Narikoravas is an embodiment of one of the most stark forms of exclusion.

### Social Exclusion and Caste

Another dimension of social exclusion that is of central importance in India is the caste system. This is in some sense the most potent form of exclusion because this sociological characteristic is fixed at birth and is completely inflexible. Though the Nariokaoravas belong to MBC group, they are worse than the SC group of people in India with all the ramifications of exclusion in every aspect of life.

### Social Exclusion and Social Justice

Social exclusion is fundamentally about inequality for it implies that there are individuals or groups that are "included". Thus it is also at bottom a notion that directly addresses the question of social justice. Any system of social or economic organization that gives rise to categories of individuals or groups that are excluded and included, would fail the elementary test of justice or fairness. On the other hand, if there is a historical legacy of long years of exploitation or oppression perpetuated against some individuals or groups, then one may legitimately justify a pattern of development that improves the condition of the oppressed to the exclusion of other better-off groups. In other words, exclusion may be justified only if the pattern of development were to help only those who are already socially and economically excluded.[48]

Hence we may sum up stating that the concept of social exclusion is a) Multi-dimensional implies deprivation in a wide range of indicators of living standards; b) Dynamic implies that people are excluded not just because of their current situation, but also because they have little prospect for future; c) Purely a relative concept in the sense that even within a country, interpretations of social exclusion/inclusion can co-exist or shift, offering different characterization of the boundary between the 'excluded' and 'included'; d) Has an agency dimension in the sense that it lies beyond the narrow responsibility of the individual concerned; e) Relational in nature in the sense that it implies a major discontinuity in the relationship of the individual with the rest of the society, inadequate social participation, lack of social integration and lack of power (Tsakloglou and Papdoulous, 2002).[49]

Exclusion is manifested in number of ways and it is multifaceted in nature and manifestations. In 2001, in an effort to standardize the measurement of social inclusion, the European Union adopted a list of social exclusion indicators known as Laeken indicators. It includes 18 statistical indicators, which cover four dimension of social exclusion such as financial poverty (income), employment (labour market) health and education.

The concept of social exclusion has also broadened its ambit to identify, define and characterize the marginalised. Besides, it has also taken into consideration the regional variations in defining exclusion i.e., those who are considered excluded in one region need not be the same in other regions. However certain sate groups, tribes, HIV affected, transgender, refugees, nomads like Narikoravas, certain religious groups and physically challenged etc., are considered castaways from the fast track of development and do not easily find their level crossing in today's 'incredible' India. Moreover one has to keep in mind the importance of temporal and special limitations while identifying the excluded. Hence the concept of social exclusion becomes an 'umbrella concept' which incorporates and implies a number of indicators of disadvantage, inequality and discrimination.'

## CONCEPT OF ENTITLEMENT

The notion of entitlement refers to the actual or effective empowerment of a person to trade his original endowment of labour power with other incomes for food and other basic necessities. Thus it is not the total production of basic necessities that would make a material difference to the inherent health or strength of a community so much as the distribution of this total amongst the population. Thus the concept of the entitlement lends itself rather appropriately to address the question of social and economic exclusion in a wider context.[50]

Entitlements are essential because they enable individuals to gain control over goods and services and particularly those that may be thought of as basic goods. Once they are armed with this, individuals are then able to enhance their capabilities to realize their full potential. A large entitlement or purchasing power allows a wider range of choices to an individual, 'which leads to extended entitlements, rights of access to resources that are socially sanctioned, although not legally binding'.[51] The phenomenon of social exclusion may then be understood as one where there are sections of the population whose entitlements are limited or negligible.

It is important to think of entitlement as not just economic entitlement, but also political and social entitlements. In a privilege-laden or feudal society, the later forms of entitlement are denied to all except a small minority of elite groups. Thus it is only an equitable distribution of economic, social and political entitlement that may be said to have the ingredients of a just society.

## THE THEORY OF EQUITY

The peoples of the world live in a situation of extraordinary inequalities and the same differ both within and across countries. Even the basic opportunities for life itself are disparately distributed. Equity is a difficult concept with a history of different interpretations, varying by country and academic discipline. Plato's *Republic* and Aristotle's *Politics* have spoken about it. It is central to most of the world religions as well.

'Equity is defined in terms of two basic principles: The first, is equal opportunity: a person's life achievements in succeeding economically, socially or politically, should be determined primarily by his or her talents and efforts, rather than by predetermined circumstances such as race, gender, social and family background or country of birth. The second principle is the avoidance of absolute deprivation in outcomes, particularly in health, education, and consumption levels. So societies may decide to intervene to protect the livelihoods of the needy members (below poverty line) even if the equal opportunity principle is upheld.

The distribution of wealth is closely correlated to social distinctions that stratify people, communities and nations into groups that dominate and those that are dominated. These patterns of domination persist because economic and social differences are reinforced by the overt and covert use of power. Such overlapping political, social, cultural and economic inequalities stifle mobility. They are hard to break because they are closely tied to the ordinary business of life. They are perpetuated by the elite, and often internalised by the marginalised or oppressed groups, making it difficult for the poor to find their way out of poverty. Inequality traps can, thus, be rather stable, tending to persist over generations. Such staggering inequalities in opportunity are intrinsically objectionable, and almost every culture, religion and philosophical tradition has developed arguments and beliefs that place great value on equity for its own sake.'[52]

## INEQUALITY TRAPS

Why do inequalities of opportunity persist, if they are both unfair and inimical to long-term prosperity and how do these inequalities reproduce themselves? The short answer is that political systems do not always assign equal weights to everyone's preferences. Policies and institutions do not arise from a benign social planner, who aims to maximize the present value of social welfare. They are the outcomes of political economy processes in which different groups seek to protect their own interests. This is rightly explained in the figure below.

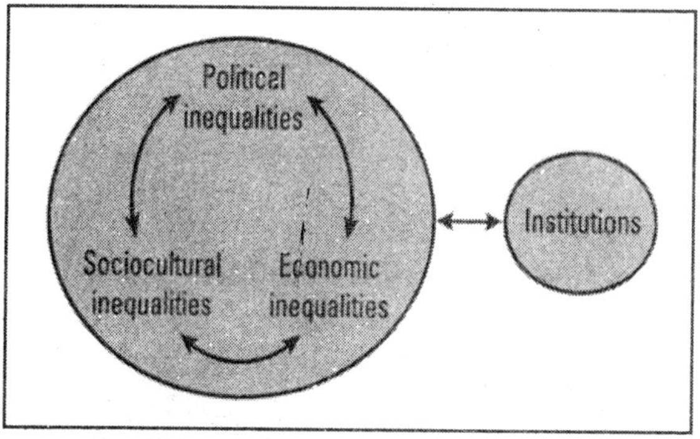


**The Interaction of Political, Economic, and Socio-cultural Inequalities**

These unequal social and economic structures tend to be readily reproduced. If a woman has not been educated and has grown up to believe that "good decent" women abide by existing social norms, she is likely to transmit this belief to her daughters and possibly to her daughters-in-law. So an inequality trap may thus prevent generations of women from getting educated, restrict their participation in the labour market and realize their potential as individuals.

Similarly, the unequal distribution of power between dominant and subordinate groups helps the rich maintain control over resources. Economic institutions are themselves embedded in unequal social and cultural institutions. The social networks that poor have access to, are substantially different from those the rich can tap into. A poor man's social network may be geared primarily toward survival, with limited access to networks that would link him to better jobs and opportunities.

Social networks are closely allied with culture that deals with relationships among individuals within groups, among groups, and between ideas and perspectives. Subordinate groups may face adverse 'terms of recognition', the framework within which they negotiate their interactions with other social groups. This would be so because, even with genuine equality of opportunities, one would always expect to observe some differences in preferences, talents, effort and luck. The real issue would be mainly for their influence on absolute deprivation and their role in shaping opportunities.

Further, equality of opportunity should focus on the distributions of assets, economic opportunities and political voice, rather than directly on inequality in incomes. Hence policies can contribute to the move from an "inequality trap" to a virtuous circle of equity and growth by leveling the playing field through greater investment in human resources of the poorest; greater and more equal access to public services and information; guarantees on property rights for all; and greater fairness in markets.

Greater equity would also imply more efficient economic functioning, reduced conflict, greater trust, and better institutions, with dynamic benefits for investment and growth.

The history of the 20th century is littered with examples of ill-designed policies, pursued in the name of equity that seriously harmed-rather than spurred-growth process by ignoring individual incentives.

Direct quantification of inequality of opportunity is difficult, but one analysis of Brazil provides an illustration. Earnings inequality in 1996 was divided into one share attributable to four predetermined circumstances that lie beyond the control of individuals-race, region of birth, parental education and parental occupation at birth-and a resid
share. These four circumstances account for arou
quarter of overall differences in earnings betwe
Arguably, other determinants of

predetermined at birth but not included in this set- for example, gender, family wealth, or the quality of primary schools. Because such variables are not included in the inequality "decomposition," the results here can be seen as lower-bound estimates of inequality of opportunity in Brazil.

Unfortunately, predetermined circumstances determine more than just future earnings. Education and health are of intrinsic value and affect the capacity of individuals to engage in economic, social, and political life. Yet children face substantially different opportunities to learn and lead healthy lives in almost all populations, depending on asset ownership, geographic location, or parental education, among others.[53]

## WHY DOES EQUITY MATTER FOR DEVELOPMENT?

The first reason is that the interconnections and resilience of the inequalities imply that some groups have consistently inferior opportunities-economic, social, and political-than their fellow citizens. Most people feel that such egregious disparities violate a sense of fairness, particularly when the individuals are affected can do little about them. This is consistent with the teachings of political philosophy or religious leaders. There is also experimental evidence suggesting that many-but not all-people behave in ways consistent with a concern for fairness, in addition to caring about how they fare individually.[54]

These inequalities will take place, firstly, with imperfect markets, inequalities in power and wealth that translate into unequal opportunities, leading to wastages of productive potential and ... secondly, economic ... inequalities that ... with impaired in... of econom... attributed ... stitutional ... and politica...

## LEVELLING THE ECONOMIC AND POLITICAL PLAYING FIELDS

One manifestation of the greater participation of the poor in economic growth is the fact that the growth elasticity of poverty reduction falls with greater income inequality. In other words, the impact of (the same amount of) growth on poverty reduction is significantly greater when initial income inequality is lower. On average, for countries with low levels of income inequality, one percentage point growth in mean incomes leads to about a four percentage-point reduction in the incidence of \$1 per day poverty. That power falls to close to zero in countries with high-income inequality. Policies that lead to greater equity lead to lower poverty, directly through expanding the opportunities of the poor and indirectly through higher levels of sustained development.

Hence an equity lens adds two new perspectives to development policymaking:

- First, the best policies for poverty reduction could involve redistributions of influence, advantage, or subsidies away from the dominant groups.
- Secondly, the dichotomy between policies for growth and policies specifically aimed at equity is not satisfactory.

This is so because, (i) economic policies are determined within a socio-political reality and hence how these policies are designed, introduced or reformed matters much (ii) public action in leveling the economic and political playing field hinges on domestic policies like investing in human capacities, expanding access to justice, land and infrastructure and also promoting fairness in markets and (iii) turns to be policies for greater global equity, in terms of access to markets, resource flows and governance.

In this process, firstly, redistributions from richer and more powerful groups that face more limited opportunities are sometimes necessary and should be pursued. Secondly, when considering policy tradeoffs between equity and efficiency, the long-term benefits of equity -including on the development of better and more inclusive institution- need to be taken into account. Thirdly, all categories of economic policy both - micro and macro- have effects on both efficiency (and growth) and equity (and distribution).[55]

## AGENCY AND EQUITY: INEQUALITIES OF POWER

'A recent study of inequalities in governance in four slums of Delhi found that access to formal government by slum dwellers is more available to the better off and to those who have good contact networks. Community leaders in these slums facilitate access primarily to their caste members, and slum dwellers are more likely to delegate custodianship of their interests to better-educated community leaders. The study concludes that because access to bureaucracy and political representation for slum dwellers in Delhi is largely the preserve of the better off and better connected, decisions of formal policymakers do not seek to represent slum interests as a whole, producing interventions that do not target those in most need.'[56]

## INTERNALISATION OF DISADVANTAGED AND INEQUALITIES OF AGENCY

Internalisation of disadvantaged leads to pernicious forms of agency that perpetuate inequalities. From inequalities in agency come inequalities in power, voice and self-confidence. Inequalities of agency are as much products of dominant institutions as sources of those institutional arrangements.

Recent work on urban slum dwellers in India suggests that a key form of powerlessness for the poor involves living with "negative terms of recognition". This concept highlights the conditions and constraints under which the poor negotiate the very norms that frame their social lives. Being so routinely treated with contempt by government officials, employers, and fellow citizens - and encountering such enormous obstacles to advancement - means that excluded groups can, over time, come to subscribe to norms about themselves and their situation whose social effect is to further diminish their dignity, exacerbate their inequality, and deepen their lack of access to material goods and services.

Hence in these circumstances, "the poor are not only persistently and overtly discriminated against. Their problems are further compounded and consolidated by their apparent complicity in it. It was revealed that their "adaptive preference" for menial occupations and ascription to norms and subservient behaviours that only legitimize and perpetuate their powerlessness. Dire material circumstances, rational expectations about their limited prospects for upward mobility, and strong beliefs about the legitimacy and immutability of their situation conspire to create a vicious circle from which it may be very difficult for the poor to escape".[57]

## LINKAGE BETWEEN RURAL AND NONFARM INCOME AND POVERTY

There is sizeable documentation on the great heterogeneity of nonfarm activities in the developing countries. This sector is neither uniform nor homogeneous set of activities. Their classification would be as follows.

### High-and-low Return Activities

'Since unskilled labour is one asset most poor households possess, and because many return to nonfarm activity due to shortage of land and capital, returns to labour in nonfarm activities become a crucial determinant of its potential contribution to poverty reduction.

Returns to labour vary markedly across nonfarm activities. Hossain (1984) documents a six-fold difference in value added per worker in rural Bangladesh across occupations such as coir rope and mat making on the one hand, and activities such as tailoring, dairying, and sugar processing on the other.

Employment in different types of nonfarm activities is not uniform across the population. Hossain (1984) documents far higher rates of employment of rural Bangladeshi women in those occupations and cottage industries where value added power is low. Lanjouw and Stern (1998) show evidence from a detailed village study in North India that while the relatively highly paid nonfarm jobs only sometimes require special skills and levels of education, employment in such jobs is concentrated among those villagers with more years of schooling, who come from high-ranked castes and have significant networks of contacts outside the village.'[58]

## A FEASIBLE THREE-WAY BREAKDOWN

'Many of nonfarm activities are seasonal and earnings often accrue via piece rate contracts rather than fixed wages or derive from self-employment rather than wage employment. Thus, nonfarm activity can be broken into

- Casual nonfarm wage employment
- Self-employment or home enterprise activities
- Regular salaried employment.

Participation in these sub sectors may thus often be the consequence of push factors, and one would consequently not expect poverty levels in this sub sector to be particularly low. Self-employment and own-account activities represent the second category of participation in the nonfarm sector. Here one is likely to observe residual, last-resort, "push" activities such as private medical practices.

According to National Council for Applied Economic Research (NCAER) survey data from 1993-94, it was observed that incomes from casual wage employment are spread narrowly around a relatively low average income level. Nonfarm self-employment earnings are somewhat higher on average than earnings from the other forms of nonfarm employment measured and have a rather fat positive tail, indicating some occurrence of high incomes. This observation is even more pronounced in the case of salaried nonfarm income. Here earnings are higher, on average, than from casual and self-employment activities, the result of a high frequency of households reporting particularly high nonfarm salaried incomes.'[59]

## EMPIRICAL EVIDENCES

According to an FAO study (1998) and Lanjouw and Shariff (2004), in rural India nonfarm incomes account for about 30 to 40 per cent of total income in all rural income quintiles. In rural

Ecuador, enterprise income is very strongly correlated with consumption quintiles, while labour incomes are more evenly distributed across quintiles. In India it can be clearly seen that while self-employment and home enterprise activities are fairly distributed over the income distribution, nonfarm casual labour incomes accrue mainly to the rich. At all-India level, the pattern observed is quite similar to that presented for Tamil Nadu.

In many countries, the probability of being poor is appreciably lower among households that partake in certain categories of nonfarm activity. In these cases, the inverse association that may arise between poverty and nonfarm incomes sometimes serves as a foundation for the argument, that expansion of the nonfarm sector can have an important beneficial impact on poverty,[60] and considered as route out of poverty.

**The Rural Nonfarm Economy as a Safety Net**

'The nonfarm sector serves an important safety net function in rural areas by providing employment-even if poorly remunerated-that helps to prevent vulnerable section of society from sliding further into poverty. There has long been a practice in many developing countries of providing workforce programmes in rural areas to mitigate the adverse distributional consequences of macroeconomic or agro climatic shocks. Dreze (1990) attributes much of post independence India's general success in avoiding widespread famine in the face of numerous droughts and crises to the introduction of such programmes. In their article Foster and Rosenzweig (2004) provides a theoretical exposition of how nonfarm and farm economy interact, built on the heterogeneity of nonfarm activities in rural areas to bring about general equilibrium relationships. They argue that a key distinction has to be made between traded and non-traded goods and services. Their study highlighted the fact that growing rural based export-oriented manufacturing sector can be expected to have an important pro-poor impact in rural India, possibly more significant than that expected from agriculture-led growth.'[61]

'Extensive research along these lines in the recent years by Datt and Ravallion using state level panel data set spanning about 40 years, came to the conclusion that poverty in India fell with higher farm yields, development spending, and nonagricultural output and that poverty rises with higher inflation.

Yet, another study by Kijima and Lanjouw in 2005 showed that poverty falls significantly with increases in agricultural daily wage rates and rises with growth in agricultural wage employment shares. An increase in agricultural wage rates of 10 per cent is associated with a 4 per cent fall in poverty, while a 10 per cent increase in the percentage of population employed as agricultural laborers is associated with 1.6 per cent increase in the poverty head count rate. Thus, they concluded that a rise in agricultural wage rates helps to reduce overall poverty levels. Besides, there was little evidence that an expansion of nonfarm employment had an important direct effect on poverty. This did not mean that nonfarm sector was unimportant for poverty reduction. Rather, expansion of nonfarm employment, particularly the unskilled casual employment opportunities that appear to present the poor with fewer barriers to entry, may play an important role in putting pressure on agricultural labour market and in raising agricultural wage rates.

In a study by Lanjouw and Shariff (2002), it was found that rural nonfarm wage income was twice as important as self-employment income in a national sample, both for the average household and for the poorest quartile. However, the average household earned only a quarter of its nonfarm wage income from casual nonfarm labour versus three quarters for the poor quartile, indicating that uneducated poor households relied on low-skill, low-entry barrier labour.'[62]

## LOP-SIDED INDIAN ECONOMIC POLICIES OF THE PAST

'That economic liberalisation and deregulation have created new sources of economic insecurity, even as they have increased exposure to long-standing vulnerabilities and failed to generate appropriate policy responses, can be seen in countries at all levels of development. It is the poorest communities, however, that are often most at risk from financial crises, natural disasters and cultural alienation. Indeed, more often than not, poverty acts to compound these threats, while for poor people, there is a dearth of effective mitigation, coping and recovery mechanisms.'[63] And India is no exception to this order.

Indian economic development has come a long way since its independence. The path of development in India and policies unremittingly pursued by the mangers of Indian state for the past sixty years and especially in the last two decades of liberalisation, has unfortunately exacerbated a situation by which the rich have become richer and the poor have sunk deep into the mire of poverty excluding the marginalsied from the share of growth that accrues to the poor. Relatively high growth rate in the GDP has remained largely inconsequential to poverty reduction and thus making nearly 720 million Indians live on Rs.20.00 per day. Poverty ratio has been declining during the recent period, but it continued to remain at very high level of 27.5 per cent (Uniform Recall Period) in 2004-05 from 36 per cent in 1993-94. The most disturbing fact was that the income inequality as commonly measured by consumption expenditure (Gini coefficient) had increased in India from 32.9 in 1993 to 36.2 in 2004 (Ali.I and J.Zhuang: 2007).

There is a wide perception that the present reform strategy is elitist-driven. Economic reforms that we have initiated are still a mixed bag till today. Its record of lifting people out of poverty is patchy at best. It is designed to help industry and corporate sector without its benefits trickling down to the poor sections of the society and leaving the rural economy untouched. The human face of the reforms is a mask not sold on the streets where majority live. Condemned to the bottom of the heap, the marginalised like the Narikoravas, see nothing to cheer for in India's so-called rise to economic superstardom.

Despite India being the second fastest growing major economy in the world after China, even with global financial crisis, the fact remains that some of the challenges that India faces are of a continuing nature. These inter alia, include eradicating poverty and illiteracy, improving its physical and social infrastructure and lastly not the least, creating employment opportunities. In consonance with these commitments to ensure faster social development and achieving inclusive pattern of growth, the government's continued focus on these initiatives are facing many roadblocks. The market economy of today has not offered safety nets to the poor like the Narikoravas, but on the contrary laid bare the fragility of economic livelihoods for these people who are at the bottom of the development ladder. The advent of globalisation has resulted in the widening of income inequality across and within countries. The rich-poor gap is not only widening, but it is doing so at an increasing pace. This has been proved by many studies in this decade.

## ECONOMIC GROWTH, A POOR INDICATOR OF ECONOMIC WELFARE

'Mahbub ul Haq was a World Bank economist who has espoused the cause of the poor and the downtrodden in the world, by stressing what he calls "Human Development" which can be quantified.[64] He hammers home the fact that there is no automatic link between increasing incomes and "flourishing human lives". While growth is necessary, as it seems to be the obsession of Indian planners today, it is not a sufficient condition for tackling poverty. It can lead to well-being only if society makes conscious effort to achieve the objective. This new paradigm, according to him, "embraces every development issued including economic growth, social investment, people's empowerment, provision of basic needs and social safety nets, political and cultural freedoms and all other aspects of people's lives.

Developing countries, which have done better at removing poverty, improved social provisions substantially, even with low per capita income levels. Most did so before opening up their domestic markets. In other words, they aimed at broad participatory growth."[65]

But the scenario is totally different in India even after 60 years of independence. According to the latest U.N. Development Programme Report, India's Human Development Index rank for 2009 was measly 134 among 182 countries. (The rankings are based on life expectancy, education enrolments, literacy and GDP per person adjusted for purchasing power). India's ranking has been pushed down from the previous years, exposing the poor quality of life in spite of a burgeoning economy.

A UNICEF report of June 2009 warned that despite several years of breakneck growth, India falls far short in protecting its own people from poverty. Some 230 million Indians suffer from chronic hunger, a number that is the biggest in any country and swelled thanks to the global downturn and sharp swings in the price of food and fuel.[66]

"A recent World Bank study says that the loss of human potential due to under nutrition would lead to a GDP loss of 2-3 per cent and can lead to 10 per cent reduction in lifetime earnings. Also, the nutrition related factors are responsible for 50 per cent of the 2.1 million under-5 deaths in India each year".[67]

There are very few countries in the world with lower levels of child nourishment. It is a situation of manifest injustice though we have the wherewithal to remove it but there is a certain level of smugness about India's achievements. As A.K. Sen puts it, "the most difficult and nasty thing about malnourishment is that it incapacitates the mind and debilitates the body."[68] "In the Global Hunger Index (2008), India ranked 66th among the 88 countries surveyed by the International Food Policy Research Institute (IFPRI). It came below Sudan, Nigeria and Cameroon and slightly above Bangladesh. In the UNDP report of 2009, India was ranked 88 among 135 countries on the Human Poverty Index (HPI). The ... nutritional emergency has to be shared by the ... and poor implementation ... of the right-to-

incomplete. It is directly linked to the right to life enshrined in the Constitutions.[69]

With continuing economic global downturn, coupled with rising food prices, will accentuate income inequality and affect employment opportunities of low-income groups disproportionately, calling for cautious policy decisions. It is one illustration of the lopsided nature of economic growth where the gains of faster growth have been captured by the privileged. In this highly stratified country, the poor for their part barely manage to continue their slow exit from hunger and misery.

It is often argued that rising inequality is the price of economic dynamism, which may be misleading in states like Kerala, Himachal Pradesh and others. Nevertheless worldwide experience proves that the poor do not automatically benefit from higher economic growth rates. Our efforts to break the poverty-insecurity trap will require a policy framework that not only generates higher growth but also revisiting how investment strategies adopted by both public and private sectors address the underlying vulnerabilities which expose households and communities to larger downside risks.

Today, India's international credit rating and the sentiments of the bullish stock market coupled with the size of economic growth rate, receive far more attention in economic policy making than lives of its poor.

## INCLUSIVE GROWTH, STILL A DISTANT DREAM

The concept of 'inclusive' growth as strategy of economic development received attention owing to the rising concern that the benefits of growth have not been equitably shared. This must be understood as a process of including the excluded agents whose participation is essential in the very design of the development process and not simply as welfare targets of development programmes.

Hence economic growth without being inclusive does not yield dividends to every section of the society and the trickle down theory does not sink well with modern concept of growth where grinding poverty is an unacceptable price of modernization. It must encompass human development and economic and social mobility for all sections of the society, and in particular, for the disadvantaged and marginalized population groups of the society. "The main operational objective is to devise long-term poverty reduction strategies for addressing these root causes of chronic poverty through a mixture of measures that not only target the vulnerabilities leading to economic security, but also allow better management of risk through mitigation and coping measures."[70]

Michael Carter, World Bank's country director in India says that the nation occupies two worlds simultaneously. In the first, economic reforms and social changes have begun to take hold and growth has had an impact on people's lives. On the other, citizens appear almost completely left behind by public services, employment opportunities and brighter prospects. Bridging the gap between these two 'Indias' is perhaps the greatest challenge facing the country today.[71] The silver lining is the presence of a counter trend of political assertion by marginalised groups-working people, disadvantaged castes, and nomads, among others. This political awakening is the best potent to bridge the yawning gap between the haves and have-nots and usher in greater equity in Indian society.

Against the growing backdrop of increasing economic and political insecurity in interwar Europe, John Maynard Keynes called for "new policies and new instruments to adapt and control the working of economic forces, so that they do not intolerably interfere with contemporary ideas as to what is fit and proper in the interests of social stability and social justice."[72] Those words resonate and find utterance just as strongly today.

Recent campaigns for the right to food, education, work and information have brought issues of deprivation and livelihood to centre stage of Indian development process, as never before. Yet these thorny issues need to be revisited with greater commitment.

## GDP REVISITED

'Five Nobel laureates in economics Joseph Stiglitz of USA, India's Amartya Sen and three others, together with 20 prominent social scientists of world renown, presented a report in Paris on 14th September 2009, on ways to improve the measurement of economic growth and correct the deficiencies of Gross Domestic Product (GDP) indicators so as to take into account social well-being. It was a call to abandon "GDP fetishism." Mr.Stiglitz, who heads the Commission on the Measurement of Economic Performance and Social Progress, wrote in the executive summary, "It is time for our statistics system to put more emphasis on measuring the well-being of the population than on economic production". Hence growth measured as a percentage increase in GDP, which is measure of value of goods and services generated in a country, has long been seen by many as a crude benchmark, to measure market economic activity. But they are increasingly thought of as a measure of societal well-being, which they are not.'[73] The new indicators must look at issues such as environmental protection and work / life balance as well as economic output to rate a country's ability to maintain the "sustainable" happiness of its inhabitants.

'The report also argues that official statisticians should concentrate on household's incomes, consumption and wealth rather than total production. All these adjustments make a difference. In 2005, the commission found France's GDP per person was 73% of America's. But once government services, household production and leisure were added in, the gap narrowed; French households had 87% of the adjusted income of their American counterparts. It turned its attention to measures of the "quality of life" that goes beyond the command of economic resources. This approach quantified people's subjective well-being-from health, marital status and age to perceptions of corruption-divided into an overall judgment about their lives (a ladder of life score). The report also examined the well-being of future generations. Their children's human capital (skills and so forth) will depend on investment

## INEFFECTIVE DELIVERY SYSTEM

We have inherited over the years plethora of schemes that are directed to the alleviation of poverty. "Each of these schemes has its own delivery silo, all designed to deliver basic goods and services to the same set of intended beneficiaries-the poor, but so carefully insulated from the other delivery silos that there is no possibility of converging the schemes of synergising their endeavours. Each delivery system has its own set of privileged: district and sub-district officials; comprador NGOs bowing and scrapping before their babu patron; hangers-on and sycophants, all of them so richly recompensed that before they get down to any actual work 85 paise is skimmed off every rupee on the average, merely to install and keep in place the delivery mechanism. The schemes in other words, exist for themselves, little bureaucratic empires so incestuously designed that the recipient has no participation in, and has less knowledge over the very building blocks of his own life."[75] The bureaucracy assumes, from the cabinet secretary down to the meanest patwari, that because they are better educated and more paid than those they 'serve', there is no need to involve the benighted in planning or implementation. Moreover, the self-image of the bureaucracy is that they are not only more efficient but also more honest than politicians, especially low-level politicians. Besides state legislators, in particular, block every attempt at genuine empowerment through the effective devolution of functions. As long as we rely on alien and transient bureaucracy to dispassionately "deliver" development to the poor, the delivery mechanism will swallow most of the resources on just putting itself comfortably in place.

Gram Sabha, the constitutionally mandated assembly of eligible voters in every village panchayat must be made accountable to the development process. If checks and counter checks are in place, much of the leakages in the system can be curbed so that the grassroot level development can become a reality as Mahatma Gandhi said on the eve of Indian Independence. "I shall work for an India in which the poorest shall feel that it is their country, in whose making they have an effective voice." Thus, the voice of the voiceless must find utterance in all that is planned for them, to make our growth process more inclusive than ever before.

## STUDIES ON NARIKORAVAS

Other than a short note by Edgar Thurston in 1905, these people have not received any scholarly attention. It was in the early seventies, Dr. Gift Siromoney of the Madras Christian College, with the help of the students of Statistics Dept. of the college conducted a series of research projects on the life of these people and published the results of his studies in the form of monographs. Besides, few small books have come up on their economic and cultural aspects.

Mr. G. Srinivasa Varma, in his book, "Vagri Boli: An Indo-Aryan Language" (1970) has made a descriptive grammar study of their language which is known as Vagriboli.[76]

Ms. Karasur Padmabharati did one of the comprehensive studies on the Narikoravas of Tamil Nadu, titled 'Narikuravar Inavaraviyal' published in 2004.[77] It covered mainly the sociological landscape of their life with many pictorial presentations. Dr. Bhakthavatsala Bharathi has edited an elaborate study on the nomads of Tamil Nadu, titled 'Tamizhagathil Nadodigal' (December 2003) in which he has given significant place to Narikoravas of the State spotlighting their social backwardness.[78]

A booklet titled "The Problems of Narikorava Community in Tamil Nadu" (2000) highlighted the problems of the community by Sathyanandan D.Theodore.[79] This formed a part of collection of Christian literature. Mr.A.Arokiaswamy had made some attempt at the study of Narikoravas, titled 'Narikuravar Vazhvu: Or Ayvu' in his postgraduate studies in Chennai.[74] Mr. Lukas Werth, from the Institute of Ethnology, Free University of Berlin has also undertaken a research study on this people in 2004. As part of the study on the people of India and in particular Tamil Nadu, Mr. K.S. Singh has brought out some salient aspects of Narikorava community in one of the volumes of "People of India."[80]

Mr. M. Sankar, a postgraduate student of Chennai had undertaken a detailed study on the whereabouts of the

Narikoravas in the whole of Tamil Nadu from 2006 to 2008 on behalf of Tamil Nadu Pazhangudi Vagrivel Tozhilar Sangam (TAPVATS), a unit of its welfare board. He had covered the then 28 districts of the State trying to highlight the dropout children among the Narikoravas during the study period. It was an eye-opener for the policy makers in the education department to take up remedial measures to counter such large-scale problem found among them.[81] Lastly, but not the least, Mr.A.Kulandai of Maduari Kamaraj Univeriity had delved into the cultural and anthropological perspective of Narikoravas in his M.Phil dissertation titled, "Vagriyargalin Vazhviyal" in 2007.[82]

## FOOTNOTES

1. Shashi, Shayam Singh., The World of Nomads, Lotus Press Publications, New Delhi-2, 2006,p.23.
2. Mishra, P.K., and Malhotra K.C., (ed.), "Nomads in India", Proceedings of the National Seminar, Anthropological Survey of India, Calcutta-16, June 1982, p.3.
3. *Ibid* p.4
4 *Ibid.*
5 *Ibid.*, p. 10.
6. Rao, Aparna and Casmir Michael., (ed.)., Nomadism in South Asia, Oxford University Press, New Delhi-1, 2003,p.12.
7. *Ibid.*, p.12.
8. *Ibid.*, p.12.
9. Das Veena, The Oxford India Companion to Sociology and Social Anthropology, Oxford University Press, New Delhi-1, Vol, 1, 2003, p. 229.
10. *Ibid*
11. Rao, Aparna, and Casmir J. Michael,(ed.), Nomadism in South Asia, Oxford University Press, New Delhi-1, 2003, pp.22-25.
12. Khazanov, Anatoly M., "Nomads and the Outside World", University of Wisconsin Press, 1994, p.10.
13. Sudarsen, V., and Kalam M.A., The Uprooted, Displacement, Resettlement Development, Gian Publishing House, New Delhi-2, 1990.
14. Das Veena., The Oxford India Companion to Sociology and Social Anthropology, (ed.), Oxford University Press, New Delhi-1, Vol, 1, 2003,pp. 220-221.
15. Mishra P.K and Malhotra KC., "Nomands in India" (ed.), "Proceedings of National Seminar, Anthropological Survey of India," Calcutta-16,1982,p.4.

16. Dhananjayan, A., The Curse and Absolution; A Study on the Role of Origin Myths among the Nomads with Special Reference to Boom-Boom Maattukaarar community, IndianFolklore Research Jourmnl,Vol.4, No.7, 2007, p.52.
17. Encyclopaedia of Britanica, Vol. 12, 1969,p.1076.
18. *www.wikipedia.org/wiki/Roma* People
19. ______________ "Pastoral Care of Nomads in India", Panci Documentation, Bhopal, 2005,p.3.
20. *Ibid.*
21. Nagesh A., "Social Organisation and Political Process among the Narikoravas", Dept.of Anthropology, Madras University, December 1990,pp.44-50.
22. *Ibid.*, pp. 46-47.
23. Arokiaswamy, A., Narikuravar Vazhu:Or Ayvu, M.A Dissertation, Loyola College, Chennai-34,2000, pp.45-56.
24. *www.mercer.edu/sociology/Idependentprojectfinaldraft*, December 07, 2002.
25. Sen, Amartya., Social Exclusion: Concept, Application and Scrutiny, Office of Environment and Social Development, Papers No.1, Manila, 2000. p,2
26. Islam Aminul S., "Sociology of Poverty", Bangladesh e-Journal of Sociology,Vol.2,No.1.January 2005,p.4.
27. Nayak, Pulin., Social Exclusion and South Asia, International Institute for Labour Studies,Cambridge,1994, chapter 2.
28. *Ibid.*, p.2.
29. *Ibid.*, p.3.
30. *Ibid.*, p, 3.
31. *Ibid.*, p.6.
32. *Ibid.*, p.6.
33. Sen, Amartya., Development as Freedom, Oxford University Press, New Delhi-1, 2008. pp-88-89.
34. Amartya Sen, The Idea of Justice, Penguin Books Ltd, London , August 2009.
35. Deccan Chronicle, 17th August 2009.
36. Prem Singh, Godwin J,(ed.), Millennium Development Goals, Allied publisher Pvt. Ltd, New Delhi, 2009, p.37.
37. Sen,Amartya., Social Exclusion, Concept, Application and Scrutiny, Asian Development Bank, Manila 2000,pp.14-18.
38. *Ibid.*, p.45.
39. *Ibid.*, p.40-41.
40. *Ibid*
41. *Ibid.*, p.41.
42. Kaur, Gunjeet., (ed.),Reserve Bank of India Bulletin, September 2009, p.1475.
43. Sen,Amartya., Social Exclusion, Concept, Application, and Scrutiny, Asian Development Bank, Manila 2000, pp.18-22.
44. *Ibid.*, p.27.

45. General Assembly Resolution , 217A (III)
46. World Economic and Social Survey 2008, Overcoming Economic Insecurity, Academic Foundation, New Delhi-2, 2009, p.vii.
47. *Ibid.*
48. Sen, Amartya., Social Exclusion, Concept, Application, and Scrutiny, Asian Development Bank, Manila 2000,p.23.
49. Prem Singh, Godwin J.,(ed.), Millennium Development Goals, Allied Publisher Pvt. Ltd, New Delhi, 2009, pp.35-36.
50. *www.google.com.*
51. *Ibid.*
52. World Development Report 2006, "Equity and Development", A co-publication of The World Bank and Oxford University Press, New York, 2006,pp.18-19.
53. *Ibid.*, p.2.
54. *Ibid.*,pp.2-7.
55. *Ibid.*,p.23.
56. *Ibid.*,p.48.
57. *Ibid.*,.p.4
58. Haggblade, Steven., Peter B.R.Hazell, Thomas Reardon (ed.), Transforming the Rural Nonfarm Economy, Oxford University Press, New Delhi-1, 2008, p.60.
59. *Ibid.*,p.64.
60. *Ibid.*,p.70.
61. *Ibid.*,pp.74-75.
62. *Ibid.*, pp. 78-124.
63. "Equity and Development", World Development Report 2006, A Co-publication of World Bank and Oxford University Press, New York, 2006,p.34.
64. Haq, Mahbub ul., Reflections on Human Development, Oxford University Press, New York,1995.
65. The Economist, June 6,2009,p.31.
66. The Economist, June 6, 2009, p.31.
67. The Economic Times, 27th August 2009.
68. Deccan Chronicle, 9th August 2009, p.9.
69. The Hindu, 27th August 2009.
70. World Economic and Social Survey 2008, Academic Foundation, New Delhi-2, 2008.
71. India Today, December 6,2004, p.21
72. John, Maynard Keynes., The Economic Consequences of the Peace, Macmillan, London. 1919.
73. The Hindu, 15th and 16th September 2009.
74. The Economist, 19-25th September 2009.
75. India Today, 24th August 2009.
76. Varma, Srinivasa G.,Vagri Boli: An Indo-Aryan Language, Annamalai University, Annamalai Nagar,1970.
77. Karasur, Padmabharati., Narikuravar Inavaraviyal, Tamizhini,Chennai-14, December 2004.

78. Bharathi,Bhakthavatsala S., (ed.), Tamizhagathil Nadodigal, Vallinam, Lawspet, Puducherry-8, Dec 2003.

79 Sathyanandan, D.Theodore., The Problems of Narikorava Community in Tamil Nadu, The Christian Literature Society, Chennai-7, 2000.

74 Arokiaswamy, A., Narikuravar Vazhvu Or Ayvu, Unpublished M.A, Dissertation, Loyola College, Chennai-34, 2000.

80. Singh, K.S (ed.), People of India- (Tamil Nadu), Vol.XL,Part II,. Affiliate East West Press Pvt. Ltd, Chennai, 1997.

81. Sankar, M., Census of Tamil Vagris, Tamil Nadu Pazhangudi Vagrivel Tozhilar Sangam (TAPVATS), Villupuram, 2008, pp.1-19.

82. Kulandai. A., Vagriyarg7alin Vazhviyal, Unpublished M.Phil Dissertation, Maduari Kamaraj University, 2007.(Unpublished M.Phil Dissertation in Tamil language)

3

# METHODOLOGY

The research methodology adopted in the present study was broadly related to the choice of the study area, collection of data, and tools of analysis.

## AREA OF STUDY

The area covered for study was the whole district of Vellore (TN) spanning an area of several hundred square kilometers and fourteen colonies where Narikoravas were settled. Though specific time of their settlement was nct known, most of them were there for several years due to obvious reasons of trade, hunting and patta land acquired over the years. They tended to live in communities though many of them did not have roof over their heads. In some areas the land offered by the Government was rejected and they preferred to live close to areas of trade. On the whole, migration was on the wane and in fact new families came to settle in established areas making the number of settlers more and more over the years.

In order to understand the socio-economic conditions of the inhabitants in the district, it was indispensable to discover the physical features, infrastructures and social and economic institutions of the area, means of livelihood and the programmes undertaken by the Government. The description of the study specifically dealt with their family background, literacy, nature of occupations, their income and expenditure pattern and the ways and means of meetings their ends on a monthly basis.

## SOURCES OF DATA

Only primary data spanning two years, i.e., April 2006 to March 2008 were used in this study. The primary data were collected from the entire population of 473 families living in fourteen colonies spread over the length and breadth of Vellore district. Besides, secondary data were also collected from census reports, information gathered from official records on them from the district collectorate at Vellore, Most Backward Welfare Society Board at Chennai and materials collected from books, journals, articles on them from different centres in the State.

## CENSUS METHOD

In order to study the income and expenditure pattern of the Narikoravs in the district, the entire district was chosen. The study was explorative, since it was the maiden attempt of its kind to be undertaken in the State. Census method was used in this study. A pilot study was undertaken among fifteen households spread over several areas and the respondents were contacted in person and all the required information were collected in the pre-tested interview schedule. (Annexure)

## DATA COLLECTION

The following details were collected from the respondents in the district related to their family, settlement, migration, family assets, basic amenities, consumer items owned, education, health conditions, social activity, main problems, suggestions for improvement in their economic and social conditions and lastly but not the least, their saving pattern and expenditure.

## PERIOD OF STUDY

The main focus of this research was to analyze the income and expenditure pattern of the sample respondents in Vellore district between April 1, 2006 and March 31, 2008, by covering all the existing Narikorava colonies, sprouting at different pockets of the district. These two years were divided into 2 peak seasons (halves) and 2 lean seasons (halves). The lean season (half) was taken from 1st April to 30th September of 2006 and 2007 and peak season (half) was between 1st October and 31st March of 2007 and 2008. Thus four surveys were conducted from all the respondents on their income sources and expenditure patterns for these two years with four seasons.

From two these halves of peak and lean months for the two years, the average one-month of peak income and peak expenditure were calculated and computed. The first half (1 April to 30th September 2006 and 2007) was taken as lean season, for the following reasons.

- Volume of trade was very low for the respondents, while peak season was a period of good sales especially the main festive months of Pongal and Deepavali occur during this peak period. Sale of beads and other articles picked up during this season.
- April to September was considered as a dry period of the year in Tamil Nadu. So hunting during this season was also at its lowest level.

## TOOLS OF ANALYSIS

Both descriptive and quantitative tools were used for the analysis of the data. Descriptive methods of analysis like simple averages and percentages were used in this study along with graphs and diagrams for easy understanding.

## QUANTITATIVE TOOLS

### Correlation Method

For finding out the relationship between the income and expenditure of the respondents for the two years and also their relationship between the lean and peak seasons, correlation coefficient was used.

$$r = \frac{\sum xy}{\sqrt{\sum X^2 \times \sum Y^2}}$$

where,

r = correlation

$\Sigma xy$ = sum of xy where

$\Sigma x^2$ = sum of $x^2$ value

$\Sigma y^2$ = sum of $y^2$ value

$\Sigma xy$ = sum of xy value

**Correlation Matrix**

For finding the relationship between the income and expenditure of the sample respondents of the study area for the two years, correlation coefficients were calculated between the variables of income and expenditure.

**Regression Analysis**

Regression model was used to determine whether or not a relationship existed between the two years on income and expenditure; their lean and peak seasons; sources of income and expenditure; to assess the relative importance of the various predictor variables.

**T- test**

To test the difference in the income between the two years, t-test was used.

$$r = \frac{r}{\sqrt{r^2}} \times \sqrt{n-2}$$

**Basic Econometric Model for Income and Expenditure**

As known, the income of the households was determined by many different factors that were both endogenous as well as exogenous in nature. Since we did not have control over the exogenous factors, the researcher was not interested in understanding the influence of the endogenous factors on household income. This would be, not only helpful in identifying those endogenous factors that were influencing the income, but also to suggest some normative measures to increase the income of these households in the coming years.

$$Y = f(Xj) + \mu \qquad \text{..........(1)}$$

Here, 'Y' stands for 'Annual Income' of the households, 'f' is a functional form, 'Xj' stands for various factors affecting the income of the households and ' ì' stands for 'error term' or the influence of other variables affecting income but not captured in the multi-linear regression model.

In econometric equation, the researcher had derived the following equation for the above description:

$$\text{Log } Y = \alpha + \beta_1 X_1 + \beta_2 X_2 + \beta_3 X_3 + \beta_4 X_4 + \beta_5 X_5 + \ldots\ldots\ldots + \beta_n X_n + \mu \quad \ldots\ldots\ldots(2)$$

Substituting the actual variables in equation (2), one gets the following econometric model:

$$\text{Log } Y = \alpha + \beta_1 \text{ SETTLE} + \beta_2 \text{ FAMSIZE} + \beta_3 \text{ EDU} + \beta_4 \text{ OCCUP} + \beta_5 \text{ ASSET} + \beta_6 \text{ BEAD} + \beta_7 \text{ CHAIN} + \beta_8 \text{ CATAPULT} + \beta_9 \text{ FLOWER} + \beta_{10} \text{ FANCY} + \beta_{11} \text{ GARLAND} + \beta_{12} \text{ ANIMAL} + \beta_{13} \text{ BIRD} + \mu \quad \ldots\ldots\ldots(3)$$

The details of the income variables are given in Table-1.

**Table 1**
**Description of Variables for Annual Income Analysis**

| *Variable Sign* | *Description* |
|---|---|
| Log Y | The Logarithmic value of annual income |
| SETTLEMENTS (Dummy) | Area of the Settlement (healthy area -1; unhealthy area -2) |
| FAMILY SIZE | Size of the Family of the Respondent |
| EDUCATION | Number of Years of Education of the Head of Household |
| OCCUPATION (Dummy) | Occupation of the Head of the Household (non-conventional occupation -1; conventional occupation -2) |
| ASSETS | Value of Household Assets (in Rs) |
| BEADS | Sales Value of Beads (in Rs) |
| CHAINS | Sales Value of Chains (in Rs) |
| CATAPULTS | Sales Value of Catapult (in Rs) |
| FLOWERS | Sales Value of Plastic Flowers (in Rs) |
| FANCY ITEMS | Sales Value of Fancy Items (in Rs) |
| GARLANDS | Sales Value of Garland (in Rs) |
| ANIMALS | Income from Animal Hunting (in Rs) |
| BIRDS | Income from Bird Hunting (in Rs) |
| Á and β | Parameters to be estimated |
| M | Error Term |

*Source:* Computed from Primary Data

$$\text{Log Exp} = \alpha + \beta_1 \text{ FAMSIZE} + \beta_2 \text{ FESTIV} + \beta_3 \text{ LIQUOR} + \beta_4 \text{ FOOD} + \beta_5 \text{ TOBACCO} + \beta_6 \text{ OTHER} + \beta_7 \text{ MEDIC} + \beta_8 \text{ MARRIAGE} + \beta_9 \text{ POOJA} + \beta_{10} \text{ PUBERTY} + \mu \quad \ldots\ldots\ldots(4)$$

The details of the expenditure variables are given in Table 2.

**Table 2**
**Description of Variables for Annual Expenditure**

| *Variable Sign* | *Definition of Variables* |
|---|---|
| FAMILY SIZE | Size of the Family |
| FESTIVAL | Annual Expenditure on Festivals (other than Vehili Pooja) (in Rs.) |
| LIQUOR | Annual Expenditure on Liquor (in Rs.) |
| FOOD | Annual Expenditure on Food (in Rs.) |
| TOBACCO | Annual Expenditure on Tobacco (in Rs.) |
| OTHERS | Annual Expenditure on other Items like clothing, etc (in Rs.) |
| MEDICINE | Annual Expenditure on Medicine (in Rs.) |
| MARRIAGE | Annual Expenditure on Marriage Related Activities (in Rs.) |
| POOJA | Annual Expenditure on Vehili Pooja (in Rs.) |
| PUBERTY | Annual Expenditure on Girl Attaining Puberty (in Rs.) |
| M | Error Term |

*Source*: Computed from Primary Data

## Analysis and Interpretation of Data

The collected data were carefully processed, suitably consolidated and tabulated and further used for analysis. The results were carefully interpreted so as to answer all the research objectives and the same had been reported in the following chapters.

# 4

# SOCIO-ECONOMIC PROFILE OF VELLORE DISTRICT AND NARIKORAVAS

## A PROFILE OF NARIKORAVAS IN TAMIL NADU

There are large number of communities in Tamil Nadu according to Anthropological Survey of India, of which 364 are notified, 143 of them are notified as backward, 109 as most backward, 76 as SC and 36 as ST communities. Of these 364, 209 have Tamil as their mother tongue. The rest have come from other places and Narikoravas are one among them.

It is commonly known in Tamil Nadu that uncivilized people were called "Kuravas". In a landscape littered with huge number of castes, there are about 70 such types of Kuravas like Punaikuravas, Uppukuravas, Malaikuravas. But those who hunt foxes and make a living on their skin, teeth and nails are called Nairkoravas, an offshoot of Vagri family who are known under different names in various regions they live. They struggle to overcome lingering prejudices and misrepresentations about the sources of their origin. "The Vagri traditionally or hardly interact with other castes on a regular pattern in rituals or otherwise. Their myth and rituals mostly refer to the Vagri alone. Their mode of life is on the whole characterised through their marginality which in the eyes of the surrounding people is manifested by their wandering mode of life, their reputation for dirtiness, amorality and for being tricksters."[1]

**Table 1**
**Districtwise Population of Narikoravas-2008**

| *District* | *Taluks* | *Villages* | *Households* | *Male* | *Female* | *Total* |
|---|---|---|---|---|---|---|
| Ariyalur | 2 | 3 | 95 | 166 | 158 | 324 |
| Chennai | 1 | 2 | 153 | 288 | 282 | 570 |
| Coimbatore | 5 | 11 | 450 | 856 | 776 | 1632 |
| Cuddalore | 6 | 11 | 311 | 694 | 652 | 1346 |
| Dharmapuri | 1 | 1 | 32 | 65 | 55 | 120 |
| Dindigul | 2 | 4 | 187 | 432 | 311 | 743 |
| Erode | 5 | 6 | 161 | 304 | 273 | 577 |
| Kancheepuram | 7 | 12 | 522 | 984 | 972 | 1956 |
| Karur | 1 | 1 | 67 | 77 | 93 | 170 |
| Krishnagiri | 3 | 6 | 355 | 633 | 614 | 1247 |
| Madurai | 1 | 3 | 160 | 319 | 283 | 602 |
| Nagapattinam | 1 | 1 | 25 | 38 | 36 | 74 |
| Namakkal | 1 | 2 | 79 | 155 | 124 | 279 |
| Perambalur | 2 | 3 | 208 | 445 | 424 | 869 |
| Pudukottai | 4 | 6 | 414 | 805 | 709 | 1514 |
| Ramanathapuram | 2 | 2 | 115 | 217 | 190 | 407 |
| Salem | 3 | 5 | 190 | 379 | 332 | 711 |
| Sivagangai | 3 | 4 | 371 | 664 | 646 | 1310 |
| Thanjavur | 3 | 9 | 489 | 967 | 788 | 1755 |
| Theni | 1 | 1 | 86 | 176 | 181 | 357 |
| Thiruvarur | 4 | 6 | 245 | 423 | 402 | 825 |
| Tirunelveli | 2 | 2 | 211 | 370 | 365 | 735 |
| Tiruvallur | 4 | 6 | 220 | 458 | 383 | 841 |

*Contd.*

| District | Taluks | Villages | Households | Male | Female | Total |
|---|---|---|---|---|---|---|
| Tiruvannamalai | 7 | 16 | 552 | 1101 | 1027 | 2128 |
| Trichy | 3 | 4 | 575 | 1030 | 926 | 1956 |
| Vellore | 7 | 18 | 602 | 1086 | 1097 | 2183 |
| Villupuram | 8 | 21 | 667 | 1351 | 1203 | 2554 |
| Virudhunagar | 1 | 1 | 105 | 253 | 215 | 468 |
| Total | 90 | 168 | 7,647 | 14,736 | 13,517 | 28,253 |

*Source: Census of Tamil Vagris*, TAPVATS (Tamil Nadu Pazhankudi Vakirivel Thozilalar Sangam), 2008

As seen in Table-1, the real spread of this group is found throughout Tamil Nadu with the biggest contingent settled in Villupuram district followed by Vellore district. Their percentage shares are indicated in Table-2.

**Table 2**
**Districtwise Percentage of the Population of Narikoravas**

| *District* | *Households* | *Male* | *Female* | *Total* |
|---|---|---|---|---|
| Ariyalur | 1.2 | 1.1 | 1.1 | 2.2 |
| Chennai | 2 | 1.9 | 2 | 3.9 |
| Coimbatore | 5.8 | 5.8 | 5.7 | 11.5 |
| Cuddalore | 4 | 4.7 | 4.8 | 9.5 |
| Dharmapuri | 0.03 | 0.4 | 0.4 | 0.8 |
| Dindigul | 2.4 | 2.9 | 2.3 | 5.2 |
| Erode | 2.1 | 2 | 2 | 4 |
| Kancheepuram | 6.8 | 6.6 | 7.1 | 13.7 |
| Karur | 0.8 | 0.5 | 0.6 | 1.1 |
| Krishnagiri | 4.6 | 4.2 | 4.5 | 8.7 |
| Madurai | 2.1 | 2.1 | 2 | 4.3 |
| Nagapattinam | 0.03 | 0.2 | 0.2 | 0.4 |
| Namakkal | 1 | 1 | 0.09 | 1.7 |
| Perambalur | 2.7 | 3 | 3.1 | 6.1 |
| Pudukottai | 5.4 | 5.4 | 5.2 | 10.6 |
| Ramanathapuram | 1.5 | 1.4 | 1.4 | 2.8 |
| Salem | 2.4 | 2.5 | 2.4 | 4.9 |
| Sivagangai | 4.8 | 4.5 | 4.7 | 9.2 |
| Thanjavur | 6.3 | 6.5 | 5.8 | 12.3 |
| Theni | 1.1 | 1.1 | 1.3 | 2.4 |
| Thiruvarur | 3.2 | 2.8 | 2.9 | 5.7 |
| Tirunelveli | 2.7 | 2.5 | 2.7 | 5.2 |
| Tiruvallur | 2.8 | 3.1 | 2.8 | 5.9 |
| Tiruvannamalai | 6.8 | 7.4 | 7.5 | 14.9 |
| Trichy | 7.5 | 6.9 | 6.8 | 13.7 |
| Vellore | 7.8 | 7.3 | 8.1 | 15.4 |
| Villupuram | 8.7 | 9.1 | 8.8 | 17.9 |
| Virudhunagar | 1.3 | 1.7 | 1.5 | 3.2 |
| Total | 100 | 100 | 100 | 100 |

*Source:* Census of Tamil Vagris, TAPVATS (Tamil Nadu Pazhankudi Vagirivel Thozilalar Sangam), 2008

"In Tamil Nadu they are known as 'kuruvikkaran'[1] or 'narikkuravar.'[2] They are known by various names in the State. In Pudukottai, they are known as Perisu or Adi, in

Tirunelveli as Nariyakar, in Nagapattinam as Narithompan, in Kanyakumari as Murattiyan or Rattiyan, in Thanjavur as Marathian, in Trichy, Salem and Villupuram districts as Narikoravas and in Chingleput and Vellore districts as Kurivikarans.

In Puducherry, they are called as Narikoravans; in Andhra Pradesh as Nakla or Naklavandlu, Pillaikuttu Ammu; in Kolkota as Singalan; in Rajasthan as Wagri, Pakdi, Singa; in Kerala as Kurivikaran; in Karnataka as Akipikki; in Maharashtra as Patha Parthilowar; in Gujarath and M.P as Wagri; in U.P, Delhi and Orissa as Akipikki.[3] Since their roots linked to Gujarath, they are called as Wagarivel jath. As Wagri in Gujarati means kuruvi, Wagrivel jath means tribe of kurivikarans. Wagriwalo means Kurivikaran and Wagri Velvado means community of kurivikarans.[4] Other names used are Kuttiraja and Shikkari, the former signifying their affinity to forested stretches and their lordship over them. Their distinctively different culture and habits make them easily identifiable.

The Narikoravas are a nomadic community of Tamil Nadu. 'They are a class of Marathi-speaking, bird-catchers and beggars who hunt jackals. According to Thurston, the word "Narikorava" is a combination of the Tamil words "Nari" and "Kurava" meaning "jackal people" or "fox people". This appellation has been bestowed upon them due to their adeptness in hunting and trapping jackals'.[5] It is indisputable that the Narikoravas are bird catchers, hunt jackals and beg but they are not Marathi-speakers. The Narikoravas call themselves Vaghris and they speak Vaghriboli, or the language of Vaghris. The Vagri language is related to Gujarati, and their culture contains many elements of that area. The names of two of their sibs suggest some connection with Gujarath and Rajasthan. One of their sibs is Gujaratha and is suggestive of a connection with Gujarath. Besides, Baines also reports of Vaghris from Gujarath. The Gujarath Jath consists of 12 sub-castes, like Jumblo, Govinda, Raamu, Panwaar and Manikyo that worship the goddess Kali (vexli). Another of their sibs is Mewado, named perhaps after Mewar of Rajasthan. The

Mewado Jath, which consists of 9 sub-castes like Dheto, Daarkyo, Heero, Navel and Naamo that worship goddess Meenakshi (novkod). The Dhaabi are sub-divided into Datto, Mnayo, Makhro. The Seliyos have only one sub-sect, the Vithyo.

Consequently, they seem to be from the western parts of India mainly from Gujarath and Rajasthan and speakers of a dialect belonging to the Indo-Aryan stock. The Narikoravas consider themselves related to the Lambadis of Andhra Pradesh and North Arcot. They are also believed to be related to other gypsy people such as Banjaras and Domar who had originated in North India. "Fraser, an authority on the gypsies of Europe, believes that the Domar are the ancestors of the Roma people and therefore, the Narikoravas are related to the 'Roma', while Thurston feels that they are related to the Khonds of Orissa."[6]

The Mewado Jath (Nandevala) sacrifices sheep and the Gujaratha jath (Jambalavala) sacrifices buffaloes. Every member belongs to any one of the five clans. Before they deal with each other, they need to identify as a member of the clan by tattooing their goddess. A common ancestor and particular goddess identify a clan. As Sita is identified with North India, it is believed that Vaghris belonged to North. According to another legend Vaghris were warriors and they were in the army of Sivaji that lost the battle with the English. On knowing this, the Vaghris hid themselves in forests with their wives and children and survived on fruits, tubers and animals.

The Vaghris, native of Tamil Nadu are known as Nari Kuravas (Tamil, Nari = Jackal) or Kurivikarans (Tamil, Kuruvi = bird). These names have been derived from their jackal-hunting and bird-catching activities. Vaghris also live in Andhra Pradesh. They are known by the Telugu people as 'Nakkalvandlu' meaning jackal people and also as "Yeddu Marugu Vetagandhu" (meaning hunters who hide behind bullocks for they conceal themselves behind bullocks while hunting. According to Thurston, they are also known as Jangal Jali or Kattu Marathi - Hindustani Paradhi or Mir

Shikari. The Vaghris are also distributed in Gujarath and Central India. They are known as Vaghris in Gujarath and in Central India they are known as Baghris. The Vaghris_of Tamil Nadu and Andhra Pradesh are however distinct from the Vaghris living elsewhere. The term Narikoravas is henceforth used to distinguish them from Vaghris who are native to other places.[7]

## LEGEND BEHIND THEIR ORIGIN

Legend behind their origin is very interesting. Once upon a time there were three brothers, one of whom ran away to the mountains and mixed with Kanakkuravans and became degraded. The descendants of the second brother were Lambadis and those to the third Kurivikarans. The lowly position of the third brother is attributed to the fact that the three brothers while wandering about came across Sita, the wife of Rama, about whose personal charms they made remarks and laughed. This made her angry and she uttered the following curse, "Malitha Shikar, naithe bhikar", thus condemning them to be hunters if they found the game and be beggars if they did not.

According to the manuals of North Arcot district, there is variant legend about the origin of Narikoravas. It says that many years ago in Rajputia, there lived two brothers, the elder of whom was dull and the younger one smart. One day it so happened they were driving a bullock along the parts by the side of a pool of water when they saw Sita bathing. The younger one hid behind the bullock, while the elder was stupid to conceal himself when the goddess had observed them. The goddess was annoyed and she ordered the elder to make a living by carrying goods about the country on bullocks, while the younger was ordered to catch birds by means of two shares, which she obligingly formed from her hair plucked from under her arm. Consequently, the descendants of the second brother who are called Narikoravas never share that portion of the story.

There is another legend according to which there was difference of opinion between two princes viz., Dharman and

Durodhana. To avoid conflict Dharman on his own exiled himself from the country. His lover went in search of him. To avoid recognition, she disguised herself as woman prophesying about the future. At that time she found out Dharman and lived with him and gave birth to a child. The descendant from this birth is called Kuruvikaran.

According to another legend, they are believed to be descendants of the Maratha warrior Sivaji who seemed to have used tigers' nail hidden in his body to attack his enemies. "Wagh" in Marathi means tiger and Wagri means those belonging to tiger tribe. Yet another legend says that losing the battle in Sivaji's army, they seemed to have thrown away their clothes and started wearing leaves and living in the forests as free people without any subjugation even of Muslim rulers. After the arrival of the British in India, these people who were expert hunters of wild animals with bows and arrows were offered guns to make their both ends meet.[8]

The Narikoravar do not remember the place of their origin, but they have apparently lived in Tamil country for several generations. It was only during the time of Mr.Kamaraj as Chief Minister of Tamil Nadu that they were given separate houses for themselves in patta land, starting from Irayur in Peramblur district. Nomads as they were, this was a temporary haven for them as most of them sold their property and moved out.

Their own language Vagriboli, is related to Rajasthani, Marathi and Gujarathi. It is believed that they originally migrated from Rajasthan to avoid persecution and conversion. They profess to be descendants of Guru Dhinarao, their patriarch who lived nearly fifteen centuries ago. The Narikoravas speak Vagriboli among themselves. They speak Tamil, Telugu or Hindi with others. They do not have a script of their own. The educated among them used to write in Tamil.

These nomads live in groups and move to various places as a group. Each group has its own leader whose position is not determined by heredity but according to his physical strength. The leader is considered to be a teacher, doctor, and judge. He is called "Kurun Matto." The leader plays a dominant role at the time of festival. He enforces discipline and imposes fines on guilty people and fines are levied in kind. Women are generally active and quarrelsome. They have dominant character over their male members and they fight more vigorously than men.

Narikoravas are considered parasites. They do not do hard work. A place where there is much to eat is considered to be a paradise for them. They have little idea of time, proportion and measurement and are superstitious about childbirth, fertility, food and sickness. Their tribai customs sometimes have the force of law based on the belief of charms and curses. They admit the falsity of their fortune-telling. They betray little shame, curiosity, surprise or grief and show no solidarity.

## NARIKORAVA COMMUNITY

The phrase "Narikorava" stands for the members belonging to Narikorava community. "According to C.Mahendran, the founder of Narikoravar Educational and Welfare Society, there are about three lakh Naikoravas in Tamil Nadu."[9]. But according to a latest quasi census study on this group by Sankar, there are around 29,000 Narikoravas in Tamil Nadu. They are also hunters of animals that inhabit the forests of the State.[10] The Narikoravas are distributed throughout Tamil Nadu and many of them living in abject poverty are often castigated for being dirty and lazy. They are known as Oosikoravar because the ban on hunting had propelled them to sell needles (oosi) and beads. Though they were a nomadic tribe for several centuries, most of them now live in permanent settlements.

Before Indian independence, the Narikoravas lived like nomadic tribes. During the British rule, they were classified under denotified tribes. After independence, they were included in the backward class list, even though they lived in caves and on the hills. Even in modern times, they are stuck in their old mould often portrayed in a bad light. Because of the lack of education and rampant poverty, they are ostracized by the society even today. This can be visualized by the way the State Government particularly in Tamil Nadu has settled them in forlorn areas of the districts. Perhaps the most important problem that keeps Naikoravas out of the social mainstream is the lack of personal hygiene.

The adults' reluctance to take up continuous work commitments and plan for the future, adopting a kind of fatalism instead, children's impatience to stick to school timetables, intolerance for rules and discipline, the tendency not to separate time and place are all examples of space-time incongruence in their itinerant life.

They live on the roadside, surrounded by filth, bath infrequently and defecate in the open. As a result, most of them suffer from gastroenteritis, foot worm, skin problems, diarrhoea and asthma even though they may not openly acknowledge them in public.

These Narikoravas zealously guard their culture, customs and traditions. They go to various places and get acquainted with new life and new customs stoutly resisting complete assimilation. They have retained a substantial part of their original language and culture without being corrupted by modern life.

## NARIKORAVAS, A CASTE OR TRIBE?

Tribe, caste, sect and class are various categories of social stratifications found in India. A tribe is collection of families or groups of families, bearing a common name, members of which occupy the same territory, speak the same language and observe certain taboos regarding marriage, profession or occupation and have developed a well-assessed system of reciprocity and mutuality of obligations.

A tribe is ordinarily an endogenous unit, the members of which confine their marriage within the tribe. Several classes constitute a tribe each of which claims kinship between the members belonging to it, based either or totomistic division, territorial contiguity or common residence. A tribe is a political unit in the sense that the tribal society owns a political organisation, either recognizes hereditary tribal chief or the several sections of it welded into a territorial group ruled by class chiefs of hereditary kings.

Tribes, caste, sect and class are used synonymously and therefore, many castes are described as tribes and many tribes have been described as castes. It is difficult job to separate groups as castes and tribe. Some sociologists and anthropologists define tribes as a social group speaking a common dialect. Perry observes "tribe is group speaking a common dialect and inhabiting a common territory". Imperial Gazette defines tribe as "collection of families bearing a common name, a common dialect, occupying or professing to occupy a common territory and is not usually endogamous, though originally it might have been so." [11]

## NARIKORAVA, A DE-NOTIFIED TRIBE

De-notified and nomadic tribes (DNTs) are an integral part of the Indian society. Each DNT community is an endogamous group. Though they are termed as tribe, for all practical purposes they are treated as castes in the traditional rural society. They are mainly patriarchal community with tribal council and strong ecological connections.

De-notified tribes were previously identified as criminal tribes. During the British rule in India, they were placed under Criminal Tribes Act 1871, and hence stigmatized for a long time. It was only in 1952 when the de-notification order was passed that they were termed as de-notified though the stigma continues. Therefore, the issue of including them as a group did not arise when the schedules were prepared in 1950.

Hence DNTs suffer from a variety of handicaps because of their exclusion from the constitutional schedules. They are covered under the Scheduled Tribes (Prevention of Atrocities Act 1989), under which the SCs and STs are protected. As a result, the violation of human rights cannot be addressed effectively. The second handicap is that the DNTs are deprived of central reservations and concessions although in some states they get the state facilities. In these circumstances, they are a beleaguered minority trying to eke out a living, encountering enormous obstacles that exacerbate their inequality in the society.

The third handicap is that DNT's are not enumerated separately in the decennial census as it is done for the SCs and STs. The correct estimation of DNT population, therefore, is not available.[12] Due to their unhygienic status even other communities including SC/ST are unwilling to mingle with them and always keep a distance from them. Hence it is still sobering time for them in very many ways. Though nomadic communities carried out diversified economic activities, at present their livelihoods are seriously threatened by modern process of development, which is characterized by mechanisation, urbanization, commercialization, large scale infrastructural development, growth in communication and transportation, enhanced social and spatial mobility and a shift from agrarian economy to industrial one. Hence, buffeted by the ban on hunting and illegal weapons, majority of these communities have begun to lose their livelihoods and shift towards alternate occupations. Hence, the Narikoravas, burdened by labels and notions that are associated with DNTs since the colonial period, suffer from similar fate and there has to be concerted efforts to rehabilitate them.[13]

## THEIR OCCUPATION

Though laggardly by nature, Narikoravas are good hunters and have an intimate knowledge of the habits of birds and animals. The very term Narikorava refers to their occupation of catching fox. They are adept at identifying the burrows of jackals and are also good at mining. They imitate the call of a jackal and birds and of a variety of other animals. To catch a fox, they go into the bushes and imitate the howl of the fox, which attracts them, and when they come out, they hit them with stick and kill them.

The Narikoravas use muzzle-loaders for hunting for which they set out in groups ranging from two or more. They rarely go alone. The men going to particular place set out together early in the morning. While hunting birds they take cover behind bushes or bullocks and as the game approaches a distance of fifty to hundred feet they fire at them, as that is the range of their weapons. During the course of hunting they disperse and regroup several times depending on the distribution of the birds and may or may not regroup while returning home.

Koravas are the ancient nomads of Tamil Nadu and they number over 70 today. Those Koravas that are engaged in fox hunting are Narikoravas. They eat their flesh and their teeth, nail and tail considered as very auspicious objects are sold for enviable price. They are good catchers of birds and harmless creatures like the rabbit, mongoose and monkey. The Narikoravas claim that they possess the horn (kombu) of the fox, which they say is present in some foxes. It is considered to be a fortune generator. They sell "Nari Kombu" or the "horn of jackal" which is used as a charm. This is manufactured by using the skin of jackal and elongated cylindrical stones. They also sell the claws of jackals and their bushy tails. They are also good taxidermists and stuff the skins of mongooses, squirrels, eagles, and foxes and sell them.

Besides, the Narikoravas catch and rear birds and animals like parrots, pigeons, moorhen, doves, hares and mongooses which they often trap and later sell them or consume them. They also hunt cats that roam around in the village and eat them.

They primarily hunt aquatic birds and koels and sell some and carry home the rest. This type of hunting of birds is carried out around the tanks of villages where the birds flock when they are full. This hunting, therefore, takes place during winter when there is water in the tanks. Another weapon they very easily make and sell is the catapult (kavan). They also trap animals and catch birds using traps and nets in the forests from where they collect herbs and plants for medicinal use. They also hunt and eat cats and if they catch excess numbers they are sold to local hotels or people who buy them in bulk. According to a recent survey undertaken by the Forest Range Officer, it was found that among the sixty who participated in a meeting near Gudiyattam, 45 had valid licenses when verification drive was undertaken by the forest department.[14]

Some of the senior Narikoravas are very good physicians. They have natural, herbal and indigenous medicines for various ailments like snake and insect bites, gas problems, paralysis, fever and headache prepared from the game and wild roots. Of late, they also use allopathic medicines, as these are available at rural health centres.[15]

These nomadic people who once eked out their living in the forests are under heavy hand of the forest regulations. They are the crossroads today, forced to choose between pursuing traditional game hunting or hawking. Over 500 gun licenses were issued in Vellore district according the licensing authority, which are being denied to young and willing hunters of today. Deprived of their traditional occupation, they are now forced to menial labour like waste paper collection and even mendicancy. It is heart-breaking to see them along with dogs search for waste food thrown out of hotels and marriage halls, thus sometimes, not having penny to their name.

Narikoravas also carry out other economic activities. They make fine bead necklaces for their use as well as for sale. This work is undertaken by young and old, of both sexes as their traditional trade, which other clans should not pick up. The women are more skilled at making them. In fact chain making comes as a hobby to them all through the day even when they see movies or when they sit around chatting.

These are sold along the sidewalks, in buses and trains along with their young children mostly at price higher than others. They go to very far off places like Patna, Agra, Varanasi and Hyderabad to buy these beads and rudrashas at cheaper rate. They get them in large quantity, process and sell them. Narikoravas are shrewd business people. They wander from town to town, village to village and sell these chains in all hues and sizes. Festivals in holy places like Tirupati, Guruvayur, Sabarimala,Velankanni and Nagore are the best occasions for them to sell their products. They spend the whole season there that lasts even three months and return to their settlements. Some even undertake foreign tours to places like Singapore, just to sell these chains, foxes' teeth and nails. Besides, they use this occasion to settle their family feuds.

They also sell combs and different types of needles, mirrors, all types of pins and knick-knacks for households. They sell needles used for repairing fishing nets, those used for stitching gunny bags, and needles used by cobblers. The needles are made of iron and are made by them, many of whom are good blacksmiths and often make good knives, usually for personal use. They share these traits with the Gadulia Lohars of Rajasthan with whom they also share other similarities pertaining to nomadic nature and the name of two of their sibs, Paawar and Dahbi, are the same as that of the clans of Lohars.

According to the exigencies of the time, they move to other jobs leaving their traditional trade because people who buy these hand-made chains are on the decline. Indeed they are good at making plastic flowers and garlands, which are easily sold in Andhra Pradesh.[16] Yet the nagging question that lingers in one's mind is, how long will they carry on with their unremunerative and unorganized trade? Hence their life encapsulates one of stricken poverty as they struggle to claw their way up to the social ladder.

## EDUCATION AMONG NARIKORAVAS

Illiteracy is rampant among these people mainly due to their nomadic life. Children are forced to join their parents, as they grapple with daily means of survival. Only recently they have realized the importance of education. Various reasons are put forth in denying admission to their kids viz., the children are unsuitable, the classes are already full or they had never any gypsy children in the school before etc. Besides, the pre-requisite for joining school is to have permanent address and it is this that the community wants to secure at the earliest. Government authorities believe that the issue of ration cards would keep them at one place and even if they shift elsewhere their movement could be tracked. Besides, the ration card would also enable them to lift their entitlement at fair price shops.[17]

## CONTEMPORARY NARIKORAVAS IN URBAN AND RURAL SETTING

Narikoravas settled in urban areas, gather waste and sell them to junk dealers besides other activities, like gathering waste papers, metals and plastic wastes, selling bead necklaces and begging. They carry out these activities throughout the year. During winter, they occasionally go to rural areas for hunting birds. Here, they also carry out their rituals, as there is no shortage of space for conducting the rituals and for accommodating the invitees in the rural expanse. They also occasionally join their kin in Andhra Pradesh. In addition, they also sell at temple fairs and festivals though this is done only occasionally.

The Narikoravas in rural areas, on the other hand carry out trade in small towns all through the year. Most of the trade is carried out in urban areas where each group of Narikoravas from the different areas has separate camping sites. They however go back to the countryside for hunting during winters when the birds flock around irrigation tanks. Those living near forest also trap wild fauna. Apart from winters, they stay in urban campsites and often make return trips to their rural settlements or travel throughout the State selling their goods. The Narikoravas living in rural areas are therefore more mobile than those living in urban areas. The latter are relatively more settled and move out very little. But those from rural as well as urban areas are fundamentally nomadic in nature despite having permanent settlements and are therefore semi-nomadic presently.[18]

## NARIKORAVA WELFARE BOARD

In order to facilitate the welfare of the community, the Government of Tamil Nadu had constituted Narikorava Welfare Board (Narikorava Nalavariyam) on 22nd May, 2008 and brought about the necessary amendment in the annual budget of 2008-09.

## INCOME AND SAVING HABITS OF NARIKORAVAS

The Narikoravas are economically backward tribe in India. The benefits of various development schemes and other facilities by the Government do not reach these people who are always on the move from one place to another. In the course of time, with better education, their upward mobility is sure to improve. Most of them live in small tents made of palm leaves, though some of them have concrete house built by the Government. Majority of them live on poramboke land.

They move to other similar places whenever they are evicted. Their hand-to-mouth existence permits them to have only bare necessities of life. Saving is not their cup of tea. They also have the accessories necessary for their occupation like nets, guns and traps though some even have T.V and cell phones. They need to hone their skills to churn out products that would have wider patronage (marketability). At present they produce and sell low-end products in busy housing colonies, bus stands, weekly markets and trains. But with certain improvement in technique and design aspects, these could capture the niche market. Once this is done, their income level would certainly go up. This is veritably seen in the products, they market these days.

Yet their struggle against daily survival is not easily winding down. Recently Narikoravas have joined Self-Help Groups (SHGs) to market their commodities. The groups especially among women at Idaya Nagar in Tirupattur have contributed to the enhancement of their daily income by the sale of wage goods.

The expenditure on special occasions necessitates savings. But the nomads hardly save any money. In fact most of the families have huge debts by their own standard. They do not trust anyone with their money and carry it in a bag wherever they go. A few families that do not move out, save paddy and grains, which they acquired during the harvest season and store them for later use. Thus, the endgame of creeping prosperity continues to be a moving target in line with their itinerant life.

On the whole they have few assets. Most of them have a few mud pots and aluminum vessels for cooking and few mats. Some of them have portable tents made of weeds that they carry wherever they go. They also have a few nets and accessories for trapping animals and birds. Most of them live in thatched house and some are even without a roof over their head. [19]

## EXPENDITURE PATTERN OF NARIKORAVAS

Major chunk of their income is spent on food. Other items of expenditure are 1. Travel 2. Clothing 3. Cinema. 4. Liquor 5. Accessories for work and trade. Each family spends about Rs.50 for their daily food, which consists mainly of rice prepared with some spices, and meat that is available to them. Clothes are bought especially for festival seasons only. Some families travel regularly and spend a small amount on that. Most of them are very fond of going to cinemas as often as they can afford. Most of the men consume alcohol regularly if they can and definitely during their festival seasons.

Besides, this most of them spend lot of their hard earned income on religious ceremonies. Pongal, Deepavali and Ayudha Pooja are celebrated by them on a small scale and around Rs.500 to Rs1000 are spent on these celebrations. More important to them are their pujas, the expenditure for which varies from Rs.500.00 for paal puja to Rs.5000.00 for Erumakkada (buffalo) puja when they sacrifice a buffalo. Their marriages also cost them anything from Rs.5000.00 to Rs.100, 000. The other occasions that involve expenditure are childbirth and death ceremonies, which are comparatively less expensive.

## A PROFILE OF VELLORE DISTRICT

Vellore district was also known as "Thondlamandlam region" in the early south Indian history. The pages of South Indian history are replete with thrilling fights for supremacy between the local chieftains and rulers on the one hand and the French and English invaders on the other. Places of historical importance in this district are Arcot, Vellore and Wallajah which have seen several small and big battles.

From the earliest times for which evidence is available, the district was part of the former Pallva Kingdom during the second half of the ninth century A.D with Kancheepuram as the capital. In the succeeding periods, the district came under the rule of Cholas, the Rashtrakutas, the Thanjavur ruler Rajarajacholan and the Hindu ruler of Vijayanagar. The district then fell under the Mohammadean Nawabs of the Carnatic, whose headquarters was Arcot. The British had introduced many socio-economic changes here in the nineteenth century. Vellore gained prominence during the freedom struggle due to the interment of many leaders.

## LOCATION AND AREA OF THE DISTRICT

Vellore district lies between 12° 15′of the northern latitude and 78° 20′ and 79° 50′ of the eastern longitude. On the east, it is bound by Kancheepuram district, on the south by Tiruvannamalai district, on the west by Dharmapuri district, on the north by Chittoor district of A.P. The total area of the district is 6,077sq.k.m. It is the fifth largest district in the State, covering 4.67 per cent of the land area.[20] Its headquarters is Vellore with important educational centres like the world famous CMC Hospital and VIT University. However the economy of the district is basically agrarian in character.

It has 3 revenue divisions, 8 revenue taluks, 52 revenue firkas and 843 revenue villages. At present there are nine municipalities, 27 town panchayats, 20 panchayat unions and 753 village panchayats as part of the local governance of the district. Apart from the local bodies, there are 12 legislative and 3 parliamentary constituencies in the district.

## SOCIO-ECONOMIC INDICATORS OF THE DISTRICT

The size and quality of population are major factors that determine regional variations in development. According to 2001 census, the population of Vellore district is enumerated as 34,77,317 comprising of 17,41,083 males and 17,36,234 females. According per population size, it is third among the

32 revenue districts of Tamil Nadu accounting for 5.6 per cent of the state population. The decadal growth of population is estimated as 15.09 per cent between 1991-2001 i.e., just above the State average decadal growth rate of 11.19 per cent.

The sex ratio in the district as per 2001 census is 997 females for every 1000 males as against the State average of 986 recording an increase from 978 of 1991 census. The density of population in the district is 572 persons per sq.km as against the State average of 478 and thus making it the ninth most densely populated district in the State.

The literacy rate in the district has increased from 60.87 per cent in 1991 to 72.36 per cent in 2001, which is lower than the state average of 73.47 per cent. Male literacy rate is 81.98 per cent and for female is 62.79 per cent.

A quick look at the occupational pattern of the people in the district shows that main workers form 33.72 per cent, of whom cultivators form 19.86 per cent of the population, followed by marginal workers in household industries as 10.02 per cent. Agricultural labourers and other workers form 88.47 per cent of the population.[21]

## FOOTNOTES

1. Lukas,Werth., "The Vagri of South India and their Ancestors", *Journal of Indian Anthropological Society, Vol.28,* 1993, p.1.
1. Moffatt, Michael., *An Untouchable Community in South India: Structure and Consensus,* Princeton,1979.
2. Beck, Brenda., *"Right and Left: Essays on Dual Symbolic Classification"*, Rodney Needham (ed.), The University of Chicago Press,1973, p.394.
3. Padmabharathi, Karasur., *Naikoravar Inavariyal,* Thamizhini, Chennai-14, 2004,p.20.
4. *Ibid,* p. 21.
5. *www.wikipedia.org.*
6. *Ibid.,*p.2.
7. Arokiaswamy, A., *Narikoravar Vazhvu, Or Ayvu,* M.A.,Dissertation, Loyola College, Chennai-34, 2000,pp. 18-26.
8. Bharathi, Bhakthavatsala S., (ed.), *Tamizhagathil Nadodigal,*Vallinam, Lawspet, Puducherry-8, December, 2003, p.7.
9. *The Hindu,* January 15, 2005.
10. Sathyanandan, Theodore D., *The Problems of Narikorava Community in Tamil Nadu,* CLS, Chennai-7,2007, p.3.
11. Xaxa, Virginius., "Tribes as Indigenous People of India", *Economic and Political Weekly,* December 18,1999, pp. 3589-94.

12. *Ibid.*, p,151.
13. *Ibid.*,p.154.
14. *Indian Express*, 29th July 2008.
15. Padmabharati, Karasur., *Narikuravar Inavaraviyal*, Tamizhini,Chennai-14, December 2004, p.9.
16. Singh, K.S., (ed.), *People of India -Tamil Nadu*, Vol XL Part II, Affiliated East-West Press Ltd , Chennai 1997, p.1093.
17. *The Hindu*, 8th January 2008.
18. *Ibid.*, p. 9.
19. Satyanandan, Theodore D., *The Problems of Narikorava Community in Tamil Nadu*, Christian Literature Society, Chennai -7, 2000.
20. *Census of India 2001*, Office of the Register General of India, New Delhi-11, Government of India Publications, 2000,p.7.
21. *Ibid.*, p. 11.

# 5

# ANALYSIS OF SOCIO-ECONOMIC ASPECTS OF NARIKORAVAS

The present study was intended to make a micro analysis of socio-economic conditions of Narikoravas particularly on their income and expenditure patterns during the financial years 1-4-2006 to 31-3-2007 and 1-4-2007 to 31-3-2008.

The present chapter attempts to make an in-depth economic analysis of the primary data collected from the two-year investigation on their entire population in the district. It was later classified, tabulated and examined.

## AREAS OF SETTLEMENT

The Narikoravas are settled all over the state in small clusters numbering over 28,000 people. Besides, some of them are also in Gujarath, Rajasthan, Maharastra, U.P and Delhi and even in Singapore. Their primary (primordial) settlements were near railway stations, bus stands, 'poromboke' lands, slums, outside theatres and other public vacant lands.

The Government and the public constantly drive them out, even though some were given houses, most of which are in dilapidated state. No specific census has been done on them so far except that they were clubbed with the MBC group. Although nomadic basically, recently these people pick up threads of the need for permanent settlement in tune with the Government's intention. This had led to the up-coming of some settlements for themselves and the researcher collected their details and the same are being presented in Table 1.

As described in Table-1, all the 14 colonies of the Narikorava families were found settled in Vellore district. The 14 colonies were (i) Agaramcherry, (ii) Alangayam, (iii) Batalappalli, (iv) Idaya Nagar, (v) J.J. Nagar, (vi) Kaniyambadi, (vii) Odagattur, (viii) Pakkam - New, (ix) Pakkam - Old, (x) Rasathipuram, (xi) Sathya Nagar, (xii) Sholingur, (xiii) T.A.W. Solur, (xiv) Vallanram. Some of them were large, while others were very small in despicable condition. A close look at these places will unveil the gravity of their misery. Agaramcherry led the list with the largest number of families (53) and the least in Alengayam (10).

**Table 1**
**Areas of Settlement by the Sample Respondents**

| *Name of the Area* | *Number of Households* | *Per cent* |
|---|---|---|
| Agaramcherry | 53 | 11.2 |
| Alangayam | 10 | 2.1 |
| Batalappalli | 36 | 7.6 |
| Idaya Nagar | 39 | 8.2 |
| J.J.Nagar | 51 | 10.8 |
| Kaniyambadi | 15 | 3.2 |
| Odagattur | 34 | 7.2 |
| Pakkam - New | 23 | 4.9 |
| Pakkam - Old | 31 | 6.6 |
| Rasathipuram | 33 | 7 |
| Sathya Nagar | 45 | 9.5 |
| Sholingur | 38 | 8 |
| T.A.W.Solur | 36 | 7.6 |
| Vallanram | 29 | 6.1 |
| Total | 473 | 100 |

*Source*: Computed from Primary Data

It was quite puzzling to note that their settlements were spread all over the district. Among the total number of fourteen settlements, the settlers arbitrarily chose five, as no sites were allotted for housing by the Government even though some areas were allotted to them for this purpose without even the minimum facilities of road, water and other basic needs that befit human dwelling. Even the allotted sites were so remote as to make them real outcasts of the society in letter and in spirit, though some of them were more than two decades old. Some dwellings were beggarly in nature, as they do not even have the roof over their heads. Hence one is nudged to believe that some settlements popped up either because of kinship among themselves, sheer convenience of the settlers or proximity to the township and hunting grounds.

## DEMOGRAPHIC PROFILE OF THE SAMPLE HOUSEHOLDS

Narikoravas were sparsely populated throughout the State just like other nomadic groups like Lambadis, Kurumbas, Boyars or other ethnic groups. The total population in the district was 2017, which was the second largest population in the State, of which male population was 987 and the rest 1030 were females. The shares of the males and females stood at 48.93 per cent and 51.07 per cent respectively.

The study had found that these people married early in life even when the bridegrooms and the brides were below the age of 21 or 18 respectively.

This sex ratio, favorable to women, went against the district level sex ratio of 1000:997. There were possible reasons for this favourable sex ratio:

- Since polygamy was being widely practised among the Narikoravas, there might be a general tendency among this community to have more female children;
- Since the bridegroom had to offer 'dowry' to the bride's family to get married, the female children were considered to be an asset. This seemed to be contradictory to other communities in general;
- The female infanticide appeared to be very low in this community due to the reason cited above as well as reasons such as, their respect for women, and the females in this community became good breadwinners of the family.

The areas of settlements of the sample households in Vellore district are given in Figure-1.

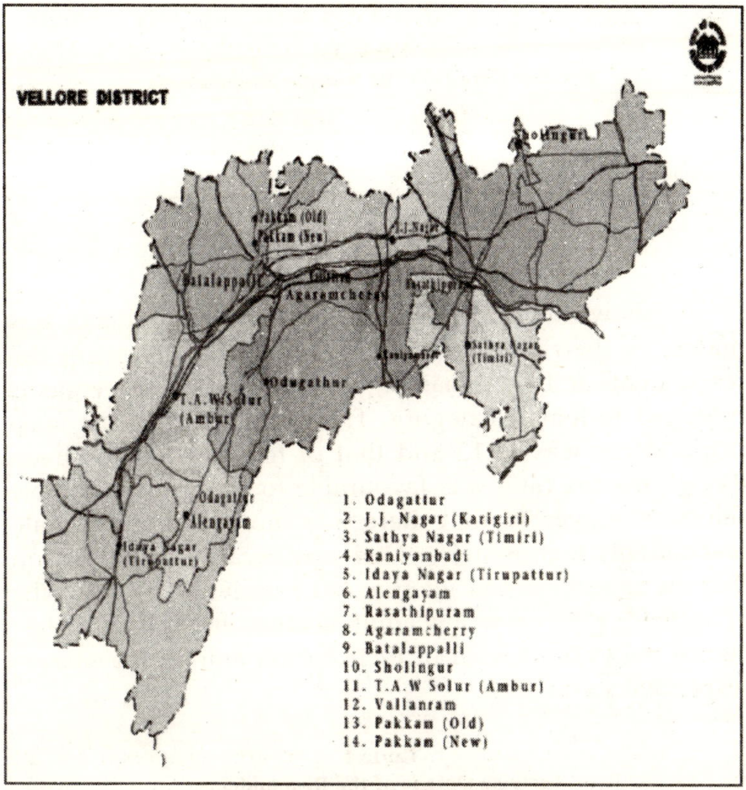


**Figure 1: Areas of Settlement**

**Table 2**
**Sexwise Ratios of the General and Narikorava Communities**

| Area | General | Narikoravas |
|---|---|---|
| India | 1000:933 | |
| Tamil Nadu | 1000:987 | 1000 : 978 |
| Vellore | 1000:997 | 1000 : 1043 |

*Source*: Census 2001 and Primary Data

As shown in Table–2, a comparative study of the presence of Narikoravas in the State vis-à-vis the general population.

It was found that men folk among them were more in the State 1000:978 (14,736:13,517), while in Vellore district, women were found more than men. i.e., 1000:1043 (987:1030).

**Table 3**
**Sexwise Details of the Sample Respondents**

| *Gender* | *Respondents* | *Per cent* | *Average Age* |
|---|---|---|---|
| Males | 432 | 91.3 | 42.12 |
| Females | 41 | 8.7 | 49.00 |
| Total | 473 | 100.0 | – |

*Source:* Computed from Primary Data

As shown in Table-3, majority of the respondents was males, as their share formed around 91 per cent of the respondents and the remaining 9 per cent of the respondents belonged to female category. The average age of the male respondents was 42.12 and that of females was 49. Even though the sex ratio was favourable to women, the sample selection suggested that there was more number of male respondents than females. This was because of the reason that the researcher had interviewed mainly the heads of the households rather than any adult members in the households. Hence the current level of distribution among the sample respondents was seen.

**Table 4**
**Agewise Details of the Respondents**

| *Age* | *Respondents* | *Per cent* |
|---|---|---|
| 1 - 30 | 130 | 27.48 |
| 31 - 40 | 151 | 31.92 |
| 41 - 50 | 84 | 17.75 |
| 51 - 60 | 60 | 12.68 |
| 61 - 70 | 31 | 6.55 |
| 71 - 80 | 14 | 2.95 |
| 81 - 90 | 3 | 0.63 |
| Total | 473 | 100.0 |

*Source:* Computed from Primary Data

As age happens to be an important socio-economic factor, its details are shown in Table-4. The study had illustrated that the majority of the respondents had been found in the age group between 1 and 40 years followed by 27.48 per cent in the age group of 1-30 years. It was quite uncommon to find old people among them due to their living through the hard grid of tough nomadic life and poor health.

Facilities available to them in and around their settlements make them vulnerable to physical ailments that would lead them to early death. However the analysis revealed that 10.13 per cent of the sample respondents had aged above sixty years.

## EDUCATION OF THE SAMPLE RESPONDENTS

Literacy level is an important socio-economic indicator of growth in any community, which can spur upward mobility among individuals, families and society as a whole. The level of education also determines the level of development of the people in a given area and there is no magic mantra second to this. Education is a great equalizer of opportunities between the rich and poor and between men and women. But the equalising promise of education can be realized only if children from different backgrounds have equal opportunities to benefit from quality education. Credit constrained households under invest in education, making the efficiency criterion more stronger for subsidizing education for the poor.

Successive governments have declared their commitment to universalizing primary and secondary education. They have not fully ensured that children born in the situations of diverse levels of wealth, caste, ethnicity and religious community, study in the same classrooms, shoulder to shoulder. A bill to this effect has been delayed far too long. It has been passed in the Parliament only in July 2009[1].

Since most of the parents were often on the move to make a living, children accompanied the adults wherever they went, which meant that completing schooling was more an exception than a rule. Besides, the social standing of these kids has pushed more children into ghettoes, prompting Government to start schools exclusively for them in few towns in the State. However, even with these arrangements, education had not picked up among them even though these kids in schools were clever and smart. Even many of the students supported by the well-wishers over the years, by way of fees and uniform, had remained as dropouts of school due to parental pressures and other obvious reasons.

Itinerant as they were, education was not a priority, much less lucrative for most of them. They preferred to eke out a living so as to make the ends meet on a daily basis and thus ward off chronic poverty. They increasingly felt the opportunity cost of education. Besides, the settlements were in remote parts of the countryside where schooling facilities were barely available and they might not have the wherewithal to support that venture as children often are considered as assets to enhance their daily kitty to support the hungry family. In view of this significance, the educational details were collected and presented in Table–5.

As found in Table–5, only 19 among 432 male members were educated (4.3%) and vast majority (95.6%) of the male heads were illiterates. Only one person had studied beyond 10th std i.e., the leader of the Idaya Nagar colony who had completed diploma in engineering. They have a long way to catch up with the district male literacy rate of 81.99 per cent. Among the 41 female heads, only 13 had done schooling between 1st and 10th standard. Thus, it was found that only 6.76 per cent of the total female respondents were literate as against the State female literacy rate of 73.45 per cent or the district literacy rate of 72.36 per cent, a sad commentary of their abysmal educational background. [2]

**Table 5**
**Details of the Education of the Sample Respondents**

| *Education* | *Male* | *Per cent* | *Female* | *Per cent* | *Total* | *Per cent* |
|---|---|---|---|---|---|---|
| Illiterate | 413 | 95.6 | 28 | 68.2 | 441 | 93.23 |
| 1st to 5th | 8 | 1.8 | 7 | 17 | 15 | 3.17 |
| 6th to 10th | 10 | 2.3 | 6 | 14.6 | 16 | 3.38 |
| 11th to 12th | 0 | 0.2 | - | - | 1 | 0.21 |
| Diploma | 1 | 0.2 | - | - | 1 | 0.2 |
| Total | 432 | 100.0 | 41 | 100.0 | 473 | 100.00 |

*Source:* Computed from Primary Data

According to a study of the census of Tamil Vagris undertaken by Sankar M. of Tamil Nadu Pazhangudi Vagrivel Thozhilar Sangam (TAPVATS), out of a total of 636 school-going children in the age group of 5-14, 432 never went to school, 153 attended schooling and 51 were dropouts. Besides 78.9 per cent of all the sons in the age bracket of 5-14, were illiterate and only one had completed diploma in engineering and a handful of boys are trying to complete high school and higher secondary education.[3]

It should be noted that the education level among the female respondents was found to be better than that of the male respondents. This gender disparity in education was seen as 96 per cent of the male respondents had been found to be illiterates while only 68 per cent of the female respondents were found be to be so. With given level of distribution of the male-female respondents, the results on the level of education suggested that in Narikorava community the females were better educated than the males. Education was considered to be a non-priority area in their life because of evident marginalisation by rest of the children in the school and these children found difficult to mix with others.

In Tamil Nadu, they belonged to the Most Backward Caste and just like their peripatetic way of life, their aspiration to be included in the list of Scheduled Tribes seemed to be running into walls for over two decades so that their progeny could get access to education and other privileges. They continued to retain a substantial part of their original language and culture without being corrupted by social mosaic of modern life wherever they went and thus resisted complete assimilation into the mainstream life in India.

## RAMPANT CASES OF SCHOOL DROPOUT

Another problem linked to migration was the prevalence of school dropout among their children that could be the reason for the abysmal literacy rate. Though the enrolment of these nomadic children was on the increase in schools, retention rates were unsatisfactory in spite of Government's allurements of midday meals, uniforms, fees, free bus pass and cycles.

Even the programmes like Sarva Shiksha Abhiyan (SSA), which is being implemented in partnership with the State Government to address the needs of children in age group of 6-14 years, has not made a dent into cases of dropout among these kids. The huge pool of school dropouts, made worse each year, was often condemned to remain economically disadvantaged, unable to change their lives for the better. In a study undertaken by Tamil Nadu Pazhangudi Vagrivel Tozhilar Sangam (TAPVATS), Villupuram in 2008, out of 341 children eligible for schooling in the district, only 73 went to school, 28 were dropouts and 240 (70.4%) never attended schooling at all, which was the highest among all the districts of Tamil Nadu.[4]

"It is widely acknowledged that the presence of a group of demoralized/disillusioned youngsters, who may have either completed schooling or have dropped out, who have little scope for employment/self-employment that yields a decent income, acts as a strong disincentive for education of other children in the family and community. Young children see the writing on the wall-education does not significantly alter the life situation of poor and the marginalised in our society. It does not lead to material gain or for that matter even unquantifiable value addition (social capital). Conversely, the presence of meaningful educational opportunities results in positive spiral and this acts as a propelling force, encouraging the community to invest in the education of their children."[5] It was quite uncommon to find a girl child completing primary school education.

There were obvious reasons for such as poverty related to insufficient income, early marriage among girls, illiteracy, parental apathy, domestic insecurity, unattractive format of education, social ridicule and seasonal migration that push a child out of the school system and eventually into the labour market. Besides, the pre-requisite for joining school was to have a permanent address. Hence school authorities did not easily admit a child if no permanent address was secured which a family ration card or voter ID could easily authenticate.

As highlighted in Table-6, it was found that the Narikorava children's nomadic character was the principal factor (56.9 %) that prevented them to stick to hard school timetables. The other reasons included (i) Parents uneducated (14.8%), (ii) no government support or scholarship (12.7%) and (iii) insufficient income (1.7%).

**Table 6**
**Reasons for School Dropouts**

| *Reasons for School Dropout* | *Number of Cases* | *Per cent* |
|---|---|---|
| Insufficient Income | 8 | 1.7 |
| Parents Uneducated | 70 | 14.8 |
| Parental Pressure | 66 | 14.0 |
| No Government Support or Scholarship | 60 | 12.7 |
| Nomadic Reasons | 269 | 56.9 |
| Total | 473 | 100.0 |

*Source:* Computed from Primary Data

Programmes for educational development, economic and social empowerment of socially disadvantaged groups and marginalised sections of the society are implemented through the State Government scholarships and free hostels. Many of these schemes are not known to the sample respondents and also even unknown to the school authorities where these kids study.

## OCCUPATION OF THE SAMPLE RESPONDENTS

The main occupation of the people, who originally belonged to the indigenous tribes, was hunting. But as they were prohibited entry into the forests to pursue this livelihood, they were forced to take up to other alternatives such as selling beaded ornaments, herbs, medicinal oil, tablets, fortune telling and singing. Thus, most of them continue to combat joblessness without ossifying their traditional livelihood. Many of them even took up to collecting waste papers and begged around for their daily livelihood though this habit was on the wane today. The mainstay of the tribe was to sell necklaces made of beads of various materials, sizes and colours, strewn on copper and silver wires. With bullion prices soaring high day-by-day, such artificial jewellery was in great demand everywhere.

Though they produced low-end goods, they continued to hone their skills to churn out products that would have wider acceptability to capture the niche market. They produced a special brand of jewellery called "Nari jewellery" that catered to fashion-conscious people and those preferred traditional forms of adornments considered them to be safe and disposable because of their affordability. Moreover it was eco-friendly because of the biodegradable materials and natural colours that went into their making. They have leveraged their chain- making skills into a profitable trade wherever they lived and whatever be the age group they belonged to.

They sourced their raw materials, mainly beads made of glass, sandalwood, clay crystal, navaratna, rudhraksha and gems from places such as Delhi, Mathura and Kolkota.

The study had found that price of a string of beads ranged from Rs.15 to Rs.800 depending on the size and quality. They even had tie-up with outlets for the sale of their products in a big way. In fact, some of them were able to sell goods of such nature to the extent of Rs.1.5 lakhs in a season.

The study had seen that majority of the sample respondents took up to hawking which fetched them better income though, meagre for their day-to-day living. The mind of the community was tuned to the extent that they were able to work on anything and everywhere because their forefathers were living itinerant life of hunting and eating animals. The details of the occupations of the sample respondents are shown in Table-7.

It was a myth to say that Narikoravas were basically known as hunters even though they were originally engaged in that trade till recently. Contrary to popular perception and as avenues of hunting get hammered, it was found that majority of the respondents (98.3%) were hawkers, even though some of them in their yesteryears were hunters, who now eked out a living all through the year by selling pins, bangles, and other knick-knacks. Some of them were making export-quality bead articles and value-added handicrafts. Only 8 of the sample households undertook hunting on regular basis and they did not go for other trades to make their ends meet and their unrelenting struggle goes on without whine or whimper.

**Table 7**
**Occupations of the Sample Respondents**

| *Occupation* | *Number of Households* | *Per cent* |
|---|---|---|
| Hawking (sale of beads, chains etc.) | 465 | 98.3 |
| Hunting | 8 | 1.7 |
| Total | 473 | 100.0 |

*Source:* Computed from Primary Data

Birds were under serious threat as the Narikoravas and landless people used catapults, country guns and nets to trap them. Hence the researcher found that this community was in a transition phase as the younger generation was least interested in perpetuating the traditional pursuit; rather they wanted to pursue education to take up regular jobs if opportunities were provided. Thus, first hypothesis was proved correct, as there was slow transition from traditional occupation to other areas of livelihood.

The real face of poverty has always a local face. The first stage of poverty eradication may be to give them a fish to eat and in the second stage to teach them to fish for themselves. This could be a sound strategy in tackling the poverty and related problems their youth face today.

A clear analysis of the contents of the Tables-5, 6 and 7 had demonstrated that there was no evidence to prove that education had helped the sample respondents positively in their upward mobility. It was also found that a lone diploma holder among the sample respondents himself was not employed in consistency with his qualification. Therefore, the conclusion was that this community had to walk miles to achieve upward mobility through education. Hence the second hypothesis stood not proved.

## TYPE, SIZE AND NATURE OF FAMILIES

It has been found that majority of the families 98.5 per cent adopted nuclear family system and the size of the family was more or less similar to a typical Indian family with slight variations in some colonies as described in Table-7. This community was patriarchal in nature and enforced traditional patriarchal structures and institutions. Nevertheless women involved in processing and manufacturing activities and forced to interact with the surrounding world on everyday basis, were bold and articulate.

Besides the size, type also was an indicator of the status of the family. Joint families (1.5%) and extended families were considered as traditional, whereas, nuclear families were considered modern. In setting up families, the Narikoravas gave importance to the nuclear type.

**Table 8**
**Type of Family of the Sample Respondents**

| *Type of Family* | *Respondents* | *Per cent* |
|---|---|---|
| Nuclear | 466 | 98.5 |
| Joint | 7 | 1.5 |
| Total | 473 | 100.0 |

*Source*: Computed from Primary Data

It was inferred that all except 7 families were nuclear mainly due to the nature of the houses occupied by them and the nature of trade they picked up. It was commonly believed that the size determined the prosperity of the family. Poor families were larger in size. It was quite possible that polygamy among men could be a cause of large families. The details of the size of the family collected from the respondents are presented in Table–8.

Among all the families, 21.4 per cent the families had two and another equal percentage had four members in their families. Only 15 families had eight or more members in their families. The average household size of all the sample households was 4.26.

**Table 9**
**Size of the Family of the Sample Respondents**

| *Size of the Family* | *Respondents* | *Per cent* |
|---|---|---|
| Single | 14 | 3.0 |
| Double | 101 | 21.4 |
| Triple | 74 | 15.6 |
| Four | 101 | 21.4 |
| Five | 71 | 15.0 |
| Six | 65 | 13.7 |
| Seven | 32 | 6.8 |
| Eight | 15 | 3.2 |
| Total | 473 | 100.0 |

*Source*: Computed from Primary Data

Concerning community leadership, it was disclosed from Table-9, that majority (78.2%) of the families followed patriarchal system in their households and women had only secondary role in their society.

**Table 10**
**Community Leadership in the Sample Households**

| *Community Leadership* | *Respondents* | *Per cent* |
|---|---|---|
| Patriarchal | 370 | 78.2 |
| Matriarchal | 103 | 21.8 |
| Total | 473 | 100.0 |

*Source:* Computed from Primary Data

## MIGRATION AMONG THE SAMPLE RESPONDENTS

Removing barriers to migration within and across borders had brought perceptible all-round benefits and held the potential to improve the lives of millions of poor and low skilled people throughout the history of mankind. Nearly one billion (one out of seven) people the world over are migrants. Of this, 740 million are internal migrants- almost four times as many as those who have moved internationally. "The poorest and the low skilled could benefit the most by moving, yet they face the largest barriers to movement: legal, financial and social."[6]

It was an accepted fact that Narikoravas are migratory by nature, often blighted by fate, as seen in the review of literature. Their non-regimental life had its own attendant disadvantages for upward mobility. The kinship system often determined who in the family migrated. The grandparents of the present generation had migrated first and hence the present generation was ignorant of how they had settled in the present colonies though the local governments earmarked some settlements. The details of the migratory character of the sample respondents are presented in Table–11.

The magnitude of migration among them is practically unknown or unpredictable. Their nomadic traits invariably belie the myth of unabated migration among them. The gypsy groups used to be nomads; however, they were getting settled easily in one place and no longer adopted nomadic practices and hence nomadism had almost become defunct among them. This was because of the welfare schemes such as, housing, provision of ration cards and other facilities such as, water supply, sanitation, education and others.

**Table 11**
**Sample Respondents and the Number of Places Lived in the Past**

| *Number of Places Lived* | *Respondents* | *Per cent* |
|---|---|---|
| Same Place | 450 | 95.1 |
| Another | 23 | 4.9 |
| Total | 473 | 100.0 |

*Source*: Computed from Primary Data

As explained in Table–11, it was found that 95.1 per cent of the households have remained in their present settlement areas and the rest 4.9 per cent had migrated to another place.

Both pull and push factors had operated in the case of migration among the Narikoravas. The push factors were the land for settlement, employment opportunities, hunting grounds for traditional hunters and other social problems like ostracization of this group by common people and communal clashes and tensions. The reasons for migration could be seen in Table–12.

As demonstrated in Table–12, the major reason for migration was lack of land for cultivation and settlement, followed by lack of employment opportunities to the extent of 20.5 per cent. The other reasons for their migration were lack of hunting ground (10.8 per cent) and social problems (3.2 per cent).

**Table 12**
**Reasons for Migration of the Sample Respondents**

| *Reasons for Migration* | *Number of Households* | *Per cent* |
|---|---|---|
| Lack of Land | 310 | 65.5 |
| Lack of Employment | 97 | 20.5 |
| Lack of Hunting Ground | 51 | 10.8 |
| Social Problems | 15 | 3.2 |
| Total | 473 | 100.0 |

*Source:* Computed from Primary Data

## FOOD HABITS AND HEALTH CONDITIONS OF THE SAMPLE RESPONDENTS

Nomadic life was associated with irregular and frugal meals coupled with bad health. Their dietary practices had virtually no restrictions. However, they were known for their robust physique and body constitution but the change in lifestyle, especially the loss of traditional diets, had made them vulnerable to modern ailments and diseases. They were too poor to take care of their health on daily basis and if at all they got sick, country or home-made medicines were the easiest solutions for their physical maladies. The incidence of gastro-intestinal diseases caused due to eating unclean meat had been quite high. The details related to their food habits are vital and hence presented in Table–13.

**Table 13**
**Number of Times Cooking Done a Day**

| *No. of Cooking Per Day* | *Households* | *Per cent* |
|---|---|---|
| One | 313 | 66.2 |
| Two | 141 | 29.8 |
| Three | 19 | 4.0 |
| Total | 473 | 100.0 |

*Source*: Computed from Primary Data

One of the best indicators of their grinding poverty was the way they fed themselves from their meagre earnings of the day. The above table underscored the fact that most of the families (66.2%) could afford only one cooking per day. While two times cooking was found in 29.8 per cent of the households and three times cooking was seen in the rest of 4.00 per cent of the households, the study also found that 81.2 per cent of them used idly for their breakfast and meals were often prepared for supper. What was left over of supper was often used as part of breakfast too for the next day even though hunger might not be visibly etched on their faces. Thus this finding proved to be a stunning revelation.

"Public Distribution System (PDS) is a major state intervention to ensure food security to people especially the poor. The Eleventh Five Year Plan has observed that PDS seems to have failed in making food grains available to the poor as is evident from falling levels of cereal consumption over the last two decades. PDS was redesigned as Targeted PDS (TPDS) where higher rates of subsidies were given to the poor and the poorest among the poor."[7] With public distribution system in place, it had put them at ease over what was earlier an unceasing struggle to get from one to the next, although all have not availed their ration cards in spite of the food security emerging as a significant policy option for public intervention and public demands for all and sundry.

Even though the Government gave ration cardholders 15 kilos of rice or wheat per month for a BPL family at the rate of Re.1 per kilo enough to sustain a small family, their dietary habits had not improved. It had not made significant dent on their malnutrition as found by the study. Since two-third of the households could afford only one cooking per day, it was concluded that these households were malnutritioned. Malnutrition reflected an imbalance of both macro and micro-nutrients that might be due to inappropriate intake and/or inefficient biological utilization due to the internal/external environment. It resulted in impaired cognitive and social development, poor school performance, and reduced productivity in later life leading to major threat to all- round development.

The analysis also revealed that only 2.1 per cent of them could afford chicken on special occasions. Those who hunted games used them as food or sold them in the neighbouring market for paltry amount. Details of their health condition are shown in Table–14.

**Table 14**
**Health Conditions of the Sample Respondents**

| *Health Conditions* | *Number of Cases* | *Per cent* |
|---|---|---|
| No Health Problems | 431 | 91.1 |
| Polio | 16 | 3.4 |
| Jaundice | 4 | 0.8 |
| Cancer | 7 | 1.5 |
| Heart Diseases | 12 | 2.5 |
| Other Diseases | 3 | 0.6 |
| Total | 473 | 100.0 |

*Source*: Computed from Primary Data

As given in Table-14, it was unearthed that majority of the respondents (91.1%) had been apparently healthy even though they were not found to be hygienic in their day-to-day living. Some were affected by polio and heart ailments as shown in the table.

## CHILDBIRTH, PUBERTY, BETROTHAL AND MARRIAGE OF THE SAMPLE RESPONDENTS

Childbirth was conducted nowadays in the neighbouring government hospitals even though in earlier times it was held in the bridegroom's house assisted by the girl's mother. Childbirth is a unique event in their life. Now most of them preferred to go to hospitals for delivery as their lifestyles were changing slowly. Deaths were rare events in the family and the dead were quickly buried as per their custom.

It was inferred from the above Table-15, that out of 337 households where childbirth took place, 187 households (39.5%) conducted childbirth in their own houses followed by 150 households (31.7%) in the hospitals and no childbirth was reported among 136 households (28.8%). No case of any infant mortality or maternal deaths was recorded in the survey.

**Table 15**
**Places of Childbirth**

| *Place of Childbirth* | *Respondents* | *Per cent* |
|---|---|---|
| No childbirth | 136 | 28.8 |
| Home | 187 | 39.5 |
| Hospital | 150 | 31.7 |
| Total | 473 | 100.0 |

*Source*: Computed from Primary Data

The Narikorava community was a growing community as seen from the size of the family. One-third of the births were conducted in the neighbouring government hospitals and they were ready to spend the required amount for the same as found in Table-16. Nearly 42 per cent of them spent between Rs.2001.00 to Rs.5000.00 for this purpose.

**Table 16**
**Amount Spent on Childbirth**

| *Amount Spent (Rs.)* | *Respondents* | *Per cent* |
|---|---|---|
| No childbirth | 127 | 26.8 |
| 500-1000 15 | 3.1 | |
| 1001-2000 | 83 | 17.5 |
| 2001-5000 | 196 | 41.4 |
| 5001-10,000 | 48 | 10.1 |
| 10,001-20,000 | 2 | 0.4 |
| 20,001and above | 2 | 0.4 |
| Total | 473 | 100.00 |

*Source*: Computed from Primary Data

The marriage system of the Narikoravas had varied from place to place, as marriage was a social institution that changed slowly as compared to other institutions in all societies. This was preceded by puberty ceremony that involved exchange of gifts and other expenses. The custom of bride price (dowry) was still prevalent among them. Anthropologists agreed that the primary function of a bride price was that of providing an additional economic benefit to reinforce the stability of marriage. It was either in kind or cash (Dej or dowry), paid by the kin of groom to the kin of bride because the groom gets additional hands of the bride and hence parents frequently indulged in extracting as much price as possible.

However exogamous marriage, adultery and pre-marital pregnancy were dealt with severely. The forms of penalties were often inhuman, brutal and barbaric. But prior to this, puberty ceremony would be held at the house of the would-be wife and it was more or less a family affair as revealed through the survey.

As another social function linked to marriage was the girls attaining the age of puberty. Despite its nomadic character and low economic profile, this society used to spend good sum on social and cultural functions in conformity with the typical Indian social set-up. Celebration of girls' attaining maturity is not a less important event in their life and this is seen in Table–17.

**Table 17**
**Amount Spent on Puberty Ceremony**

| *Amount Spent on Puberty Ceremony (Rs)* | *Respondents* | *Per cent* |
|---|---|---|
| No Puberty Ceremony held | 233 | 49.3 |
| 1001-5000 | 120 | 25.3 |
| 5001-10000 | 81 | 17.1 |
| 10001-25000 | 31 | 5.5 |
| Above 25001 | 8 | 1.6 |
| Total | 473 | 100.00 |

*Source*: Computed from Primary Data

As discussed in it, nearly half of the sample households (49.3%) never conducted it while 120 (25.3%) had spent between Rs.1001.00 to Rs.5000.00 for this function. The study also found that 81 (17.1%) of the households spent between Rs.5001 and Rs.10,001 and 31 (5.5%) households spent between Rs.10,001 and Rs.25,000 and 8 households (1.6%) had spent above Rs.25,001 for this function.

Functions of this nature and type also are used to bring gifts and presents and the same would be of interest to know and hence Table-18.

There was a significant percentage of households (97.9%) that had not received any money for puberty related functions. However, out of the remaining 10 households, which celebrated puberty function, almost all the households received an amount ranging from above Rs.1000.00 up to Rs. 7000.00 as gifts. The inference was that even this nomadic group was not an exception in incurring such expenses on social and cultural ceremony to keep up with the age-old customs and conventions.

**Table 18**
**Collection during the Puberty Ceremony**

| *Amount Received at Puberty Ceremony (Rs)* | *Respondents* | *Per cent* |
|---|---|---|
| No money received | 463 | 97.9 |
| 1001-2000 | 2 | 0.4 |
| 2001-3000 | 2 | 0.4 |
| 3001-4000 | 2 | 0.4 |
| 4001-5000 | 1 | 0.2 |
| 5001-6000 | 2 | 0.4 |
| 6001-7000 | 1 | 0.2 |
| Total | 473 | 100.0 |

*Source*: Computed from Primary Data

Parties of both bride and bridegroom in consultation with their community/group panchayat, often arranged betrothal ceremony, which was held in the girl's house during which the would-be bride, would be gifted with new clothes and other gifts as per Hindu tradition. The bridegroom's party would meet the entire expenses for this ceremony.

The analysis revealed that the said function was not held in about 56 per cent of the sample households and 21.1 per cent received between Rs.10,001 to Rs.20,000 gifts from bridegrooms' family, followed by 14.7 per cent received gift collections worth less than Rs.10,000. The study also found that gift collections were more than Rs.20,000 and the highest value fell between Rs.60,001 and Rs. 70,000.

**Table 19**
**Collection during Betrothal Ceremony**

| *Amount Received (Rs)* | *Number of Cases* | *Per cent* |
|---|---|---|
| No betrothals held | 264 | 55.8 |
| 0-10,000 | 70 | 14.7 |
| 10,001-20,000 | 100 | 21.1 |
| 20,001-30,000 | 19 | 4.0 |
| 30,001-40,000 | 3 | 0.6 |
| 40,001-50,000 | 13 | 2.7 |
| 50,001-60,000 | 3 | 0.6 |
| 60,001-70,000 | 2 | 0.4 |
| Total | 473 | 100.0 |

*Source*: Computed from Primary Data

A boy usually picks up the girl from nearby places for marriage. But marriage outside the clan was anathema to them. Many young girls were married off before they could reach the legal minimum of 18 years. It was often found that a goat sacrificer had to marry a buffalo sacrificer, and vice versa. This wedding ceremony among the Narikoravas was a homely affair and stretched out programme conducted lasting three days according to Hindu traditions. The marriage proposal was accepted and approved by their community panchayat including the dowry to be paid by the bridegroom. As a female child was a blessing to a family, usually the entire marriage expense was borne by the bridegroom's family.

**Table 20**
**Places of Marriage Celebration**

| *Place of Marriage Conducted* | *Respondents* | *Per cent* |
|---|---|---|
| No Marriage | 249 | 52.6 |
| House | 197 | 41.6 |
| Outside | 27 | 5.7 |
| Total | 473 | 100.0 |

Source: Computed from Primary Data

As ceremonies, social celebrations and expenses are two sides of the same coin, the Narikorava community was not an exception to this and hence the study found that no formal marriage had taken place in 52.6 per cent households, while 41.6 per cent of them had conducted marriages in their own houses under shady trees or common places as illustrated in Table-20. Marriages were held outside places too (5.7%). It was the bridegroom who offered dowry to the bride and this was done more so in cash than in kind.

As the investigation revealed, there were neither marriages nor expenses in about 49 per cent of the sample households followed by 18 per cent that had found to be spending less than Rs.10, 000 each. 12.7 per cent cases spent in the range of Rs.10,001 to Rs.20,000 and in 7.8 per cent cases, the expenses fell in the range of Rs.40,001 to Rs.50,000. The expenses went beyond Rs.50,000 in 1.5 per cent sample cases.

**Table 21**
**Expenditure on Marriages**

| *Amount (Rs)* | *Frequency* | *Per cent* |
|---|---|---|
| No Marriage | 230 | 48.6 |
| Less than 10,000 | 85 | 18.0 |
| 10,001-20,000 | 60 | 12.7 |
| 20,001-30,000 | 23 | 4.9 |
| 30,001-40,000 | 31 | 6.6 |
| 40,001-50,000 | 37 | 7.8 |
| More than 50,000 | 7 | 1.5 |
| Total | 473 | 100.0 |
| Mean Expenses | | Rs.23,763.37 |

*Source*: Computed from Primary Data

Since marriage was a protracted celebration as in other Hindu groups involving huge expenses, such expenses often went beyond their means, leading to huge debts all through their life. The average amount spent for the occasion was Rs.23,763.37. The gifts they received were not high as indicated in Table-22.

It was discovered that only 9 (2%) of the respondents who had conducted marriages for their children had received gifts in the range of Rs.1000.00 to Rs.20, 000.00 for marriages and their mean amount was Rs.10, 555.00, while about 98 per cent of the cases did not involve in any marriage gifts.

**Table 22**
**Value of Gifts Received at Marriages**

| *Marriage Gifts (Rs)* | *Respondents* | *Per cent* |
|---|---|---|
| No gifts received | 464 | 98.1 |
| 1000 | 1 | 0.2 |
| 3500 | 2 | 0.4 |
| 7000 | 1 | 0.2 |
| 10000 | 1 | 0.2 |
| 15000 | 2 | 0.4 |
| 20000 | 2 | 0.4 |
| Total | 473 | 100.0 |
| Mean Amount | Rs.10,555.00 | |

*Source*: Computed from Primary Data

Human existence was related both to births and deaths, which are not to be separated from incurring expenses. The community under survey brought out details on death ceremonies that are seen in Table-23. It was observed that though majority (60.6%) had not conducted death ceremonies, the remaining 39.3 per cent of the respondents had spent an average Rs.16,430.00, and the expenses ranged between Rs.2, 000 to Rs.100, 000.00 for the function.

**Table 23**
**Expenditure Incurred on Death Ceremonies**

| *Amount Spent on Death Ceremony (Rs)* | *Respondents* | *Per cent* |
|---|---|---|
| No money spent on death ceremony | 287 | 60.6 |
| 1000-10,000 | 97 | 20.5 |
| 10,001-20000 | 36 | 7.6 |
| 20001-30,000 | 21 | 4.4 |
| 30,001- 40000 | 10 | 2.1 |
| 40,001-50000 | 9 | 1.9 |
| 50, 001-60,000 | 7 | 1.4 |
| 60,001-70,000 | 2 | 0.4 |
| 70,001-80,000 | 0 | 0.0 |
| 80,001-90,000 | 1 | 0.2 |
| 90,001-1,00,000 | 3 | 0.6 |
| Total | 473 | 100.00 |
| Mean Expenses | Rs.16,430.00 | |

*Source*: Computed from Primary Data

Table 24
Conductor of Death Ceremonies

| *Conductor of Death Ceremonies* | *Respondents* | *Per cent* |
|---|---|---|
| No death ceremonies held | 344 | 72.7 |
| Head of the Family | 74 | 15.6 |
| Others (leader, public) | 55 | 11.6 |
| Total | 473 | 100.0 |

*Source*: Computed from Primary Data

It was customary to perform certain rituals on the occasion of death and the study also brought out that among 129 families, where deaths had occurred, 74 heads of families (15.6 per cent) conducted the death ceremonies, while in the remaining cases, the rituals were performed by others as given in Table-24.

## RELIGIOUS HABITS OF THE RESPONDENTS

Religious attitudes, beliefs and practices of the contemporary society are undergoing changes due to modernization. Similarly elements of rationality, secularism and modernity have crept into the belief systems of these people as well.

The goddesses provided the primary identification for a person as a Vagri in this nomadic society. A man was considered as a Vagri if he possessed one of their goddesses, and he might marry only a woman whose father had a different goddess than that of his own. The goddesses of the Vagri are not worshipped at permanent temples, but each man has his own portable shrine, and he has to sacrifice buffaloes or goats separately to his own goddess. Thus not only was the goddess vexli distinct from the goddess novkod, but also, one man's vexli was distinct from another man's vexli, with a separate history.

However, importance of religion in day-to-day life had not eroded. Earlier, a section these nomads thrived on these activities but now they have lost the necessary patronage. Table-25 below explains the main goddesses they worshiped.

Narikoravas on the whole were religious people mostly subscribing to Hindu religious practices and festivals even though some of them attended Christian and other festivities. Some of them attended church services too occasionally and exhibited Christian symbols in their houses. They were ready to spend huge amount of money on festivals, which landed them in debt trap all through the year.

**Table 25**
**Belief System of the Sample Respondents**

| *Gods Worshipped* | *Respondents* | *Per cent* |
|---|---|---|
| Kaliyammal | 296 | 62.6 |
| Madurai Meenakshiammal | 159 | 33.6 |
| Samundeeswari | 18 | 3.8 |
| Total | 473 | 100.0 |

*Source*: Computed from Primary Data.

As shown in the above table, majority (62.6%) of the respondents worshipped the Hindu goddess Kaliammal, followed by Madurai Meenashiammal, (33.6%) and the rest the 3.8% worshipped Samundeswari.

**Table 26**
**Main Festivals Among the Sample Respondents**

| *Main Festival* | *Respondents* | *Per cent* |
|---|---|---|
| No Festival celebrated | 2 | 0.4 |
| Karthikadeepam | 177 | 37.4 |
| Aadi | 255 | 53.9 |
| Deepavali | 39 | 8.2 |
| Total | 473 | 100.0 |

*Source*: Computed from Primary Data

**Table 27**
**Annual Expenditure on Festivals**

| *Annual Expenditure on Festivals (Rs)* | *Respondents* | *Per cent* |
|---|---|---|
| No Annual Festivals | 2 | 0.4 |
| 101-5000 | 278 | 58.7 |
| 5,001-10,000 | 75 | 15.8 |
| 10,001-15,000 | 38 | 8.0 |
| 15,001-20,000 | 30 | 6.3 |
| 20,001-25,000 | 17 | 3.5 |
| 25,001-30,000 | 9 | 1.9 |

*Contd.*

| Annual Expenditure on Festivals (Rs) | Respondents | Per cent |
|---|---|---|
| 30,001-35000 | 7 | 1.4 |
| 35,001-40,000 | 4 | 0.8 |
| 40,001- 45,000 | 2 | 0.4 |
| 45,001-50,000 | 7 | 1.4 |
| Above 50,001 | 4 | 0.8 |
| Total | 473 | 100 |
| Annual Average Expenditure of Sample HouseholdsRs.9183.51 | | |

*Source*: Computed from Primary Data

Nearly all celebrated one festival or the other during the year in a grand manner, except 0.6 per cent with spending ranging from Rs.100.00 to more than Rs.50, 000.00 and with an average of Rs.9222.00. Majority of them, 278 (58.7 %) spent around Rs.5000.00 annually for festival occasions. Festivals were great occasions for them to squander their meagre income.

## COMMUNITY LEADERSHIP, CONFLICTS AND SETTLEMENT

Each group had its own leader whose position was not determined by heredity but by his physical strength. The leader was considered to be a teacher, a doctor, a judge, and a star and called as "Kuru Matto". He played a dominant role at the time of festivals. He acted like a dispenser of justice, imposed fine on guilty people. Besides, there were also few women leaders among them as well.

**Table 28**
**Methods of Solving Conflicts**

| Methods of Solving Conflicts | Respondents | Per cent |
|---|---|---|
| Caste Council | 217 | 45.9 |
| Panchayat | 255 | 53.9 |
| Outside Panchayat | 1 | .2 |
| Total | 473 | 100.0 |

*Source*: Computed from Primary Data

Family conflicts were part and parcel of their daily living and they were resolved through various means available to them. The above Table–28, revealed that major source of resolving conflicts were through their own panchayats, (53.9%) followed by the Caste Council (45.9%).

**Table 29**
**Functions of the Community Leader**

| *Functions Community Leader* | *Respondents* | *Per cent* |
|---|---|---|
| Arrangement of Houses | 142 | 30.0 |
| Law and Order | 265 | 56.0 |
| Conducting Marriages | 66 | 14.0 |
| Total | 473 | 100.0 |

*Source*: Computed from Primary Data

Leadership in the colony was often decided commonly and there was no time frame for this. As described in Table–29, the three main functions of the community leader was (i) to maintain law and order (56%) (ii) arrangement of houses (30%) and (iii) conduct of marriages (14%).

## ASSETS OWNED BY THE RESPONDENTS

Poverty among them was conspicuous by the type of belongings they owned, although some of them liked to show off in their own style by displaying their assets.

**Table 30**
**Pairs of Dress Owned by the Sample Respondents**

| *Pairs of Dress Owned* | *Respondents* | *Per cent* |
|---|---|---|
| One | 36 | 7.6 |
| Two | 157 | 33.2 |
| Three | 124 | 26.2 |
| Four | 68 | 14.4 |
| Five | 86 | 18.2 |
| Six | 2 | 0.4 |
| Total | 473 | 100.0 |

*Source*: Computed from Primary Data

The contents of the Table-30 amply spotlighted the abject poverty prevalent in the study group. Majority (33.2%) of the Narikoravas owned only two pairs of dress followed by three pairs (26.2%) that were usually bought once or twice a year during the festival seasons from the cheapest shops in the market. Clothing followed food and shelter in the order of necessaries needed for human beings. "East or West, home is the best", as the saying goes, the need for shelter was not an exception to the sample respondents. The details are presented in Table-31.

**Table 31**
**Ownership of the Sample Households**

| *Type of House* | *Respondents* | *Per cent* |
|---|---|---|
| No house owned | 1 | 0.2 |
| Own | 204 | 43.1 |
| Rented | 28 | 5.9 |
| Allotted (built by Govt.) | 180 | 38.1 |
| Temporary Place | 53 | 11.2 |
| Waste Land | 7 | 1.5 |
| Total | 473 | 100.0 |

*Source*: Computed from Primary Data

As exhibited in Table-31, 43.1 per cent of the families had their own houses even though the idea of a house dwarfs any verbal description with just plastic sheets or coconut leaves, followed by 38.1 per cent of the households having their houses built by the Government at different places, mostly on poromboke lands at different periods and most of them were in dilapidated state, at the time of survey, on the brink of collapse at any time because they were built poorly with minimal investment. Those living in makeshift shelters had hardly anything over their heads as roof, constantly exposed to vagaries of nature and living in stark poverty and squalor. They were consistently making strong pitch for decent houses to end their nomadic life. Permanent stay in a particular place supported by ration card or election ID, had jeopardized their attempts at securing Government houses. However, unfazed by minimum requirements and plagued by daily penury, they are compelled to skimp on many necessities of life. It was also found that 5.9 per cent lived in rented houses also, while makeshift arrangements of tents in temporary places had been seen in 11.2 per cent cases. The nature of their dwellings is shown in Table-32.

**Table 32**
**Nature of the Houses Owned by the Sample Respondents**

| *Nature of the House* | *Respondents* | *Per cent* |
|---|---|---|
| Kutcha | 86 | 18.2 |
| Thatched | 130 | 27.5 |
| Tiled | 160 | 33.8 |
| RCC | 97 | 20.5 |
| Total | 473 | 100.0 |

*Source:* Computed from Primary Data

As revealed by the survey, there were four types of houses such as (i) kutcha (ii) thatched (iii) titled and (iv) reinforced concrete constructions and their shares were 18.2 per cent, 27.5 per cent, 33.8 per cent and 20.15 per cent respectively.

Hunting was one of the traditional occupations of the Narikoravas even though it was on the wane as the Government had imposed break on this. In order to curb the mindless poaching of animals and birds, in particular around lakes and rivers, the Revenue Department had been asked not to issue new gun licenses or renew the old ones to those indulging in hunting.

**Table 33**
**Ownership of Guns by the Sample Households**

| *Own Gun* | *Respondents* | *Per cent* |
|---|---|---|
| Yes | 206 | 43.6 |
| No | 267 | 56.4 |
| Total | 473 | 100.0 |

*Source*: Computed from Primary Data

It was learnt that there were nearly 500 gun licenses issued by the Vellore District Licensing Authorities. As discussed in Table-33 only 206 (43.6%) said that they owned their own guns and 267 (56.4%) of them were licensed for two years and many a youngster kept illegal guns, fending off Government warnings. Though many possessed guns, they were often hidden in their own houses. The details of the value of the guns are indicated in Table-34.

**Table 34**
**Value of Guns Possessed by the Sample Households**

| *Value of Gun (Rs)* | *Respondents* | *Per cent* |
|---|---|---|
| 2000 | 26 | 12.6 |
| 2500 | 61 | 29.6 |
| 3000 | 119 | 57.7 |
| Total | 206 | 100.0 |

*Source*: Computed from Primary Data

It was revealed that about 58 per cent had stated that the value their guns was each priced at Rs.3000.00, about 30 per cent valued at Rs.2500 and the rest at Rs.2000.00.

Lack of access to resources or assetlessness is a unique characteristic of poverty of the sample households in all its manifestations. This was amply demonstrated in the number of household assets they possessed. Yet mobile phones and motorbikes, which were initially perceived as niche products, had now changed the landscape. Their assets are given in Table-35.

**Table 35**
**Assets Owned by the Sample Respondents**

| *Assets* | *Yes* | *No* | *Total* |
|---|---|---|---|
| Motorbikes | 37 (7.8) | 436 (92.1) | 473 (100) |
| Bicycles | 159 (33.6) | 314 (66.4) | 473 (100) |
| Fans | 96 (20.3) | 377 (79.7) | 473 (100) |
| TV | 140 (29.6) | 333 (70.4) | 473 (100) |
| Radio | 166 (35.1) | 307 (64.9) | 473 (100) |
| Gas Connection | 9 (1.9) | 464 (98.1) | 473 (100) |
| Phone/Cell | 37 (7.8) | 435 (92.0) | 473 (100) |
| Furniture | 38 (8.0) | 435 (92.0) | 473 (100) |

*Source*: Computed from Primary Data
*Note*: Figures in brackets represent rowwise percentages.

As portrayed in Table-35, the sample households had possessed minimum assets. The conspicuous one was motorbikes possessed by about 8 per cent and other items were not of much value and those items were not owned by around two-thirds of the sample population.

The survey also revealed that most of the households owned only bare minimum number of cooking utensils and hardly two plates. Only two families kept livestock and poultry for their own use. One kept a flock of sheep reared by his family members. Thus, it was concluded that their resource-base was poor. It could also be inferred that their nomadic character also caused them to hold minimum items so that their mobility could be easy.

## PASTIME AND RECREATION

The study found that only 19.9 per cent of them read newspapers or magazines. It was also learnt from the respondents that 72.9 per cent of them went for movies regularly. 79.9 per cent of them said that they preferred to go by bus than by cycle. In case they happened to travel by train 71.7 per cent of them did not buy ticket. Those who possessed TVs, and radio sets, either watched or listened them also. The inference was that the Government's free distribution of colour T.V set did not reach them due to their mobility and non-availability of ration cards.

## INFRASTRUCTURE FACILITIES

Narikoravas lived on the fringes of the society and their settlements were often away from mainstream life and livelihood because of Government apathy over the years making them to live in abject conditions, though availability of public goods would enhance their living standard and welfare. Such details are given in Table-36.

**Table 36**
**Infrastructure Facilities Available to the Sample Households**

| *Infrastructure Facilities* | *Households' Access* | *Per cent* |
|---|---|---|
| Public Taps | 202 | 42.7 |
| Borewell | 100 | 21.1 |
| Common Well | 62 | 13.1 |
| Tank | -101 | 21.4 |
| Pond | 8 | 1.7 |
| Electricity connections | 271 | 57.3 |
| Toilet facility (wet) | 33 | 7.00 |

*Source*: Computed from Primary Data

From the Table-36, it was learnt that 42.7 per cent had common tap water from common tank built by the Government. Only 57.3 per cent had electricity connections at home for which most of them paid service charges though the earlier beneficiaries do not pay as they still managed with single connection in their homes.

With a culture of unsettled life, though the trend was on the decline in the recent years, they lacked the basic infrastructure facilities and lived in appalling and squalid surroundings. 95.7 per cent of them threw their disposable wastes in the open air as majority of them did not have their own land and they were unhygienic by nature due to obvious reasons like lack of water for drinking and bathing.

Coming to the area of toilet facilities, 93 per cent of them used open ground to answer their nature's call. Most often women had to wait for darkness for this purpose. Even if toilets were constructed in the recently built houses, they remained unused.

## SALE OF PRODUCTS

Though this community was engaged in variety of economic activities such as bead making and sale of simple household articles, their trade was often threatened by modern process of development chararacterised by mechanization, urbanization and commercialization. Majority of this community had begun to lose their livelihood and begun to shift towards alternate occupations. However, what they produced was often sold in neighbouring towns and religious centres like Sabarimala, Tirupathi, Velankanni, Mahabalipuram and other places.

The uncertainty of sales and income pose serious challenges to a life on the margins. Besides, their vistas of opportunities to earn income primarily by hawking remained unorganized. They remained largely as small players without organisational or marketing channels/skills, unsupported by the Government. They did not work in concert with private companies that could buy their goods. In relation to this, Table-37, was prepared and presented.

**Table 37**
**Places of their Products Sale**

| *Products* | *Respondents* | *Per cent* |
|---|---|---|
| No Sale | 93 | 19.7 |
| Neighbouring Towns | 245 | 51.8 |
| Cities | 121 | 25.6 |
| Pilgrim centres | 4 | 0.8 |
| Not Applicable | 10 | 2.1 |
| Total | 473 | 100.0 |

*Source*: Computed from Primary Data

It was learnt that majority of them (51.8 %) sold their products in the neighbouring towns, followed by their sales in cities to the extent of 25.6 per cent. It was also found that 46.1 per cent of them stocked their products to a maximum period of three weeks. The other source of income for these people was income from their traditional trade of hunting both animals and birds, even though this trade was rapidly shrinking due to several restrictions by the Government and the society at large.

## INCOME FROM HUNTING (ANIMALS AND BIRDS)

Although they were originally hunters by tradition, this trade was dwindling due to Government restrictions. It was found that only 1.7 per cent of the respondents was engaged in hunting small animals and birds as seen in Table-38.

Looking at the individual type of hunting, one would get some interesting results. In the case of hunting of animals, the mean monthly income stood only at Rs.520.08, which was less than the mean value of combined income from hunting (animals and birds) which was Rs.543.33 per month. The mean value of income from bird hunting was Rs.454.41, which was lesser than the overall mean income from hunting. Hence the researcher concluded that hunting of both animals and birds was better than birds alone.

Thus, observing income from hunting alone, it was discovered that it offered additional earning to the family kitty, as this income was combined with the rest of items in the monthly income calculation. For the regular eight

**Table 38**
**Monthly Income from Hunting–Animals and Birds in the Sample Households**

| *Details* | *Number of Households* | *Range (Rs.)* | *Minimum (Rs.)* | *Maximum (Rs.)* | *Sum (Rs.)* | *Mean (Rs.)* |
|---|---|---|---|---|---|---|
| Income from Hunting: Animals | 127 (26.84%) | 1400 | 100 | 1500 | 66050 | 520.08 |
| Income from Hunting: Birds | 34 (7.18%) | 2950 | 50 | 3000 | 15450 | 454.41 |
| Income from Hunting Animals and Birds | 161 (34.02%) | | | | | 543.33 |

*Source*: Computed from Primary Data.
*Note*: Figures in brackets represent percentages of the sample households

respondents who were engaged in hunting, it did not offer any kernel of hope for comfortable livelihood.

## BORROWINGS AND SAVINGS

The variety of activities as livelihoods was astonishing for an ordinary Narikorava family and not all of them were satisfactory and remunerative. No additional sources of finance were kept in place to bolster their private income. Hence finance is an important input for income generation and upward mobility. Besides, banking is the kingpin of all economic activities both for individuals and economies. It is instrumental in shaping the destiny of an individual who needs to come up in life. Banks and financial institutions are catalytic agents to accelerate income generation and can make a significant contribution in eradicating poverty and unemployment. So a closer scrutiny of their financial security, which is hinged on borrowing, is imperative.

There are two types of borrowings, viz., benign and pernicious borrowing. Borrowing from friends, relatives or fellow villagers on the basis of altruism or reciprocity may be an example of the benign type of traditional security arrangement. On the other hand, usurious borrowing from local moneylenders (in exchange for collaterals) is an example of the pernicious type of traditional security arrangement.

Traditional security arrangements of the benign type are few and the very prevalence of the later type among these people was a proof of inadequacy of the benign type.

Most of the Narikoravas borrowed for various reasons at the rate of Rs.6 for every Rs.100 or Rs.60.00 for every Rs.1000.00 per week, which worked out to be between 160 to 172 per cent per year. Hence the story of Narikorava family in raising minimal resources was a sad commentary of their earning as highlighted in Table 39.

**Table 39**
**Sources of Borrowing of the Sample Households**

| *Sources of Borrowing* | *Respondents* | *Per cent* | *Maximum Amount (Rs.)* |
|---|---|---|---|
| Commercial Banks | 5 | 1.05 | 45,000.00 |
| Co-operative society | 7 | 1.47 | 35,000.00 |
| Traders | 30 | 6.34 | 100,000.00 |
| Relatives | 188 | 39.7 | 50,000.00 |
| Moneylenders | 170 | 35.9 | 150, 000.00 |
| Friends | 2 | 0.42 | Not Known |
| No Borrowings | 71 | 15.01 | |
| Total | 473 | 100.00 | |

*Source*: Computed from Primary Data

The above Table-39, underscored the fact that only 5 of the respondents had borrowed from the banks up to a maximum of Rs.45, 000.00; 7 of the respondents had borrowed from co-operative banks to a maximum limit of Rs.35,000.00; 30 of the respondents had borrowed from traders to a maximum limit of Rs.1,00,000.00; 188 of the respondents had borrowed from relatives to a maximum limit of Rs.50,000; and 170 of them had borrowed from usurious money lenders to a maximum of Rs. 1,50,000 and only two had borrowed from their friends. Thus a sound mixture of both benign as well as pernicious type of traditional security arrangements existed among them to entrap them all through life. It was found that only 71 respondents (15.01%) did not borrow from any sources. Thus, on the whole it was ascertained that burgeoning debt had limited their economic maneuverability.

"The poor are often prevented from securing access to formal savings programmes through a mixture of unfamiliarity, distance, paucity and the indivisibility of available saving instruments in the formal banking sector. Alternative savings institutions/programmes that are more suited to the needs and capabilities of poor households can remove such barriers and allow those households to save and use their savings as a means of coping with risks. Hence savings are often a better form of self-insurance and it can generate an "income effect."[8]

**Table 40**
**Saving in Bank/Post Office for the Sample Households**

| *Saving in Bank/ Post Office (Rs)* | *Respondents* | *Per cent* |
|---|---|---|
| Nil | 460 | 97.3 |
| 250 | 1 | 0.2 |
| 500 | 1 | 0.2 |
| 1000 | 1 | 0.2 |
| 1200 | 3 | 0.6 |
| 1300 | 1 | 0.2 |
| 1500 | 1 | 0.2 |
| 1800 | 1 | 0.2 |
| 2000 | 3 | 0.6 |
| 8000 | 1 | 0.2 |
| Total | 473 | 100.0 |

*Source*: Computed from Primary Data

Hence coming to the area of saving, it was found that only 13 of them had savings in the bank/post office to a maximum limit of Rs.8, 000 i.e., no savings with co-operative banks, friends or relatives. Thus, it was concluded that savings were practically alien to these people who lived in abject poverty.

## SOCIAL SUPPORT SCHEMES LIKE OLD AGE PENSION, MATERNITY BENEFITS AND SELF-HELP GROUPS

There are varieties of welfare schemes that benefit the poor in every society. Narikoravas are beneficiaries of cash transfer programmes of the Governemnt like old age pension, widow's pension and maternity benefits. In general, advocates of cash transfer programmes point to their ease of disbursement, low administrative costs and ability to reach the poor directly and bolster their self-esteem and productive capacity.

According to an important result in economics, pioneered by economists Jadish Bhagwati and late V.K. Ramasami, the least costly way to achieve an objective is to employ a policy that directly targets it. Accordingly, the least costly policy to give immediate relief to the poor is direct cash transfer to them, not National Rural Employment Guarantee Scheme (NREGS) launched by the Government that assures 100 days of employment to one adult in each rural household at the statutory minimum wage.

Some researchers had pointed out these programmes had demerits too, among which were promotion of idleness and dependency, and potentially distortionary and discriminatory effects, as well as their proneness to corruption. Despite these drawbacks, programmes of such cash transfers had never dwindled in Tamil Nadu.

It had been found that only 10 respondents availed themselves of old age pension under the scheme that fetched each of them Rs.400.00 per month and only 2 respondents got maternity benefits from the Government and no other Government welfare measures were claimed by any of the respondents, and hence school scholarships were still on paper. Only 7 respondents gained from self-help groups. However, 206 of them received some help from panchayats. Besides, 351 (74.2%) had ration cards.

But when the researcher analysed the impact of self-help group among the respondents in the settlements, he found that only two settlements, had SHG programmes, viz., in Idaya Nagar and Agaramcherry that had some impact on their income.

Table-41, showed the average monthly incomes of the sample households during the study period. It also revealed that there was 9.8 per cent increase in the income of the respondents in Idaya Nagar from year 1 to year 2, while there was 4.35 per cent decrease in their income in Agaramcherry

**Table 41**
**Self-Help Group and the Sample Household Incomes**

| *Name* | *No. of Households* | *Mean Monthly Income of 2006-07 (Rs.)* | *Mean Monthly Income of 2007-08 (Rs.)* | *% Change in Income* |
|---|---|---|---|---|
| Agaramcherry | 53 | 2426.13 | 2320.56 | - 4.35 |
| Alangayam | 10 | 1075.00 | 1680.50 | +56.32 |
| Battalapalii | 36 | 2462.78 | 2313.19 | - 6.07 |
| Idaya Nagar | 39 | 2379.36 | 2612.95 | + 9.81 |
| J.J.Nagar | 51 | 1792.64 | 2073.43 | + 15.66 |
| Kaniyambadi | 15 | 1045.00 | 1552.50 | + 48.56 |
| Odagathur | 34 | 2402.94 | 2123.53 | - 11.62 |
| Pakkam - New | 23 | 1244.56 | 2060.87 | + 65.59 |
| Pakkam - Old | 31 | 2045.32 | 2691.93 | + 31.61 |
| Rasathipuram | 33 | 2082.57 | 2051.13 | - 1.50 |
| Sathya Nagar | 45 | 3432.78 | 2068.44 | - 39.74 |
| Sholingur | 38 | 2268.42 | 2168.42 | - 4.40 |
| T.A.W.Solur | 36 | 2830.55 | 2671.53 | - 5.61 |
| Vallanram | 29 | 2292.24 | 2492.24 | + 8.72 |
| Monthly Average Income | 473 | 2282.02 | 2259.35 | - 0.99 |

where SHGs existed. Hence the third hypothesis was not proved among all the settlements of the sample respondents. It was shown that neither the involvement of self-help groups nor government agencies had catapulted their income during the study period. But on the contrary, absence of constructive programmes and populist schemes of each successive Government since 1967, aimed at consolidating their vote bank, effectively blocked the transformation of their socio-economic conditions. These programmes never made a dent in their poverty. Therefore, it is suggested that there should be need for effective Government intervention to enhance their income sources particularly through self-help groups.

## THEIR PARTICIPATION IN PUBLIC LIFE

Though the Narikoravas lived a semi-nomadic life, they participated in public life in their own way for their own good even though they lived on the periphery of common life.

As revealed in Table-42, 289 (61.1%) of them took part in the panchayat elections and 180 of them in 'Katta' panchayat

Table 42
Participation in Social Activity

| *Panchayat Functions* | *Respondents* | *Per cent* |
|---|---|---|
| Panchayat Elections | 289 | 61.1 |
| Katta Panchayat | 180 | 38.1 |
| Participation in assembly elections | 208 | 43.9 |
| *Political affiliations* | | |
| A. AIADMK | 356 | 75.3 |
| B. DMK | 117 | 24.7 |

*Source*: Computed from Primary Data

(38.1%). 221 (46.7%) of them elected their leaders in their own respective colonies. 208 (43.9%) exercised their franchise in assembly elections though parliamentary elections were alien to them. They had strong political affiliations as 356 (75.3%) of them voted for AIADMK and the rest for DMK on a regular basis.

## THEIR MAIN PROBLEMS AND WAYS TO MITIGATE THEM

The major weighty issues that confronted Narikoravas were poverty, illiteracy, discrimination and opportunities for employment. Discrimination had been their lot since time immemorial. Due to their consumption of birds and animals, tabooed by settled Hindu communities, they were classified as untouchables as per Hindu varna system and excluded from streets inhabited by upper castes. Hence their status in society was on par with Dalits and at times even lower. Due to consistent neglect by the officialdom, there had been strong protests from the community and their struggle to get ST status is long drawn.

Labelled as untouchables for generations and burdened by the daily grind of survival for a hand- to- mouth existence, Narikoravas look up to the Government and other outside agencies to alleviate themselves from the shackles of poverty through multi-pronged strategy and plethora of programmes specifically directed to them.

The main reasons for the State's failure to achieve inclusive growth and distributive justice for these people are the wrecking of the well designed community development programme that aimed at all- round development of their settlement, the lack of success in providing adequate employment opportunities at living wages to a rising population, the neglect of school education and the absence of special measures designed to help children of these people. In short, their major development imperatives have not been rightly addressed over the years.

**Table 43**
**Main Problems of the Sample Respondents**

| *Problems* | *Respondents* | *Per cent* |
|---|---|---|
| Nil | 46 | 9.7 |
| Social | 40 | 8.5 |
| Economic | 306 | 64.7 |
| Political | 76 | 16.1 |
| Cultural | 5 | 1.1 |
| Total | 473 | 100.0 |

*Source:* Computed from Primary Data

After going through a variety of problems faced by them, it was found from the above Table-43, that 306 respondents (64.7%) found their economic problems as the main cause for their unceasing backwardness and present state of affairs, as they continue to be ostracized by the society at large in very many subtle ways. Yet they soldier on overcoming many seemingly insurmountable odds. Besides, they remain outside any official affirmative action of the Government and their struggles barely merit a mention in the print or electronic media. Untouchability practised towards them by common folks, remains the biggest social malaise.

Table–44, exposed the leading laments of these people that needed to be addressed at the earliest, to emancipate them from gnawing poverty. They lived in colonies that were bereft of decent infrastructure facilities that were ordinarily available to common men as they were more often treated as third class citizens. What emerged from the above data was that their basic amenities were woefully inadequate for any respectable life as they continue to bear the brunt of Government apathy.

**Table 44**

**Facilities to Improve the Socio-Economic Status of the Sample Respondents**

| *Facilities Required* | *Respondents* | *Per cent* |
|---|---|---|
| Nil | 38 | 8.0 |
| House Facility | 17 | 3.6 |
| Water Facility | 163 | 34.5 |
| Health Facility | 137 | 29.0 |
| School Facility | 88 | 18.6 |
| Electricity Facility | 30 | 6.3 |
| Total | 473 | 100.0 |

*Source*: Computed from Primary Data

Social welfare, while giving additional weight to the income/consumption of the poor, must give importance to the access of public goods to the poor. This is due to the fact that individual welfare depended not only on private consumption but also on public goods and services supplied by the state. This was not undertaken by the State to a large extent with regard to these people. Their stark poverty is the sum total of a multiplicity of factors that include not just income and calorie intake but also access to house and credit, nutrition, health and longevity, education and safe drinking water, sanitation and other infrastructure facilities making it an unsolvable enigma as they were treated with discrimination even in getting the basic infrastructure facilities, leave alone social dignity. Majority of them 163 (34.5%) wanted water facility as their prime need followed by health care needs. (29%)

Besides, lacking the basic facilities for their existence, lack of employment opportunities stared at their faces, which was basically linked to their illiteracy. Even policymakers were often concerned with the question of whether public works programmes could be scaled up and regularised to the point that they could offer a guarantee of employment. The proscription of games hunting as well as killing of endangered species of birds and wildlife had depleted the Narikoravas of their traditional sources of livelihood and siphoned their income. As a result, unemployed Narikorava youths were taking up to crime and illegal activities besides being caught for illegal hunting and thus leading to seething discontentment among them. Some of them had been arrested for the possession of unregistered firearms, as country rifles were banned according to the Indian laws. Hence discontentment with their daily yearning for better quality of life was reverberated in their struggle to secure ST status, which would seemingly alleviate their overall poverty. But the Government is in a bind over giving ST tag.

**NEW INITIATIVES**

In 1996, a social welfare organization named Narikorava Seva Sangam was formed, in order to educate Narikorava children and facilitate them to lead a settled life. Other social welfare organisations too, had poured in their efforts to improve their lot. In May 2008, the State Government set up Narikorava Welfare Board for the Narikoravas, headed by the Backward Class Minister. They were pinning all hopes on this board to mitigate their struggles. Self-Help Groups particularly among women had sprung up all over the State to give sound footing to their economic activities. Paucity of public investment in their infrastructure needs and Government's offer of Nelson's eye to their pressing needs including housing, roads, health, credit and sanitation which would facilitate the flow of goods, financing and price information across space, had hampered their progress from time immemorial and continue to keep them at the periphery of decent living and as pariahs of Tamil society. In short, there has been a systematic failure in giving these alienated people a stake in modern economic process that inexorably intrude into their living spaces. Their poverty is a very complex phenomenon with social, economic, psychological and educational underpinnings which is much more than what meets the statistical eye.

As usual, the Government had been great on words and short on action and its lackadaisical approach to any target oriented programmes or affirmative action was much wanting even as the lives of these people continued to be mired in poverty.

## FOOTNOTES

1. *The Hindu*, 30 July 2009.
2. *Census of India 2001*, Office of the Register General of India, New Delhi-11, Government of India Publications, 2001,p.11.
3. Sankar, M., *Census of Tamil Vagris*, Tamil Nadu Pazhagudi Vagrivel Tozhilar Sangam (TAPVATS), Villupuram, 2008,pp.1-19.
4. Sankar, M., *Census of Tamil Vagris*, Tamil Nadu Pazhangudi Vagrivel Tozhilar Sangam (TAPVATS), Villupuram, 2008.
5. *The Hindu*, 9th Aug.2009.
6. *Human Development Report, 2009*, "Overcoming barriers: Human mobility and Development". Oxford University Press, New Delhi-2,2009,p.21.
7. *Economic Survey, 2008-09, Government of India*, Ministry of Finance, Oxford University Press, New Delhi-2, 2009, p.262.
8. *World Economic and Social Survey 2008*, Academic Foundation, New Delhi-2,p.164.

# 6

# INCOME AND EXPENDITURE PATTERN OF NARIKORAVAS

## THE LIST OF ITEMS OF INCOME AND EXPENDITURE

Livelihood of either the poor or the rich rests upon the quantum of expenditures incurred by households, which ultimately rest on income sources.

Items of monthly income sources for Narikoravas of Vellore district were sale of beads, chains, catapult, plastic flowers, fancy items, garland and others. Besides, income from hunting of animals and birds were also included.

Items of monthly expenditure were rice, wheat, ragi, kambu, vegetables and fruits, oil and pulses, chicken/fish, tea/coffee, liquor and tobacco (gutka). Among other monthly expenses included clothing, education, medicine, electricity and transport. Festivals, social gatherings, marriage, poojas and puberty ceremonies were also calculated separately.

## ANALYSIS OF THE RESPONDENTS' INCOME AND EXPENDITURE

### Lean Periods Income Range and Distribution of the Households during 2006-07 and 2007-08

As seen in Table-1, the majority of the respondents (30.4%) had secured an average monthly income ranging from Rs.1001 to Rs.2000.00 during the lean season of the first year

(2006-07), and the average monthly lean period income of all the respondents was Rs.2257.44.

**Table 1**
**Monthly Lean Period Income Range and Distribution of Sample Households between 2006-07 and 2007-08**

| | *Sample Respondents* | |
|---|---|---|
| *Income Categories* | *2006-07* | *2007-08* |
| Less than Rs. 1000 | 103(21.8%) | 16(3.4%) |
| Rs. 1001 - 2000 | 144(30.4%) | 171(36.2%) |
| Rs. 2001 - 3000 | 130(27.5%) | 180(38.1%) |
| Rs. 3001 - 4000 | 49(10.4%) | 87(18.4%) |
| Rs. 4001 - 5000 | 30(6.3%) | 13(2.7%) |
| Rs. 5001 - 6000 | 10(2.1%) | 3(0.6%) |
| Rs. 6001 - 7000 | 1(0.2%) | 1(0.2%) |
| Rs. 7001 - 8000 | 3(0.6%) | 2(0.4%) |
| Rs. 8001 and above | 3(0.6%) | Nil |
| Total | 473 | 473 |
| Average Monthly Income for Lean Periods | Rs.2257.44 | Rs.2429.63 |

*Source*: Computed from Primary Data
*Note*: Figures in brackets represent columnwise percentages

Besides, it had been also inferred from the same table that the average monthly lean income of the year 2007-08 was Rs.2429.63 which was slightly higher than the previous year and majority of the respondents (38.1%) had secured higher income with an average monthly income ranging from Rs.2001 to Rs.3000.00. These people attributed the possible explanation for this slight increase in the lean incomes of two years, to the volume of their turnover and better promotion of sale.

### Peak Periods Income Range and Distribution of the Sample Households during 2006-07 and 2007-08

As found in Table-2, it had been found that 145 of the respondents (30.7%) had secured a monthly income ranging from Rs.1001 to Rs.2000.00 during 2006-07, and the average monthly income of all the respondents for this peak period was Rs.2307.02.

Besides, 241 of the respondents (51%) had secured a monthly income ranging from Rs.1001 to Rs.2000.00 during the peak season of the second year reflecting an increase of 66.2 per cent in the number of respondents for the same amount as compared to the previous year, though the average monthly peak income of all the respondents had plummeted to Rs.2089.08, showing a significant shift in the income sources among these families. It was possibly answered by their capacity to market their products vigorously and also due to the seasonal and locational change in the sale of products.

**Table 2**
**Monthly Peak Income Range and Distribution of Sample Households between 2006-07 and 2007-08**

| | *Sample Respondents* | |
|---|---|---|
| *Income Categories* | *2006-07* | *2007-08* |
| *Less than Rs. 1000* | *92(19.5%)* | *37(7.8%)* |
| Rs. 1001 - 2000 | 145(30.7%) | 241(51%) |
| Rs. 2001 - 3000 | 126(26.6%) | 150(31.7%) |
| Rs. 3001 - 4000 | 58(12.3%) | 34(7.2%) |
| Rs. 4001 - 5000 | 28(5.9%) | 6(1.3%) |
| Rs. 5001 - 6000 | 14(3.0) | 1(0.2%) |
| Rs. 6001 - 7000 | 4(0.8) | 0(0.0%) |
| Rs. 7001 - 8000 | 2(0.4) | 0(0.0%) |
| Rs. 8001 - 9000 | 1(0.2) | 1(0.2%) |
| Rs. 10,000 and above | 3(0.6) | 3(0.6%) |
| Total | 473 | 473 |
| Average Monthly Income for Peak Periods | Rs.2307.02 | Rs.2089.08 |

*Source*: Computed from Primary Data
*Note*: Figures in brackets represent columnwise percentages

## Total Monthly Incomes (lean and peak) Compared between 2006-07 and 2007-08

Analysing the income secured by the respondents over the two years as a whole, the researcher found that there was a significant increase in the average monthly income of the respondents, as more people were pushed to a higher slab of income range.

**Table 3**
**Total Monthly (lean and peak) Incomes Compared between 2006-07 and 2007-08**

| | Sample Respondents | |
|---|---|---|
| *Income Categories* | *2006-07* | *2007-08* |
| Less than Rs. 1000 | 17(3.6%) | 0(0%) |
| Rs. 1001 - 2000 | 75(15.9%) | 7(1.5%) |
| Rs. 2001 - 3000 | 73(15.4%) | 67(14.2%) |
| Rs. 3001 - 4000 | 72(15.2%) | 135(28.5%) |
| Rs. 4001 - 5000 | 74(15.6%) | 116(24.5%) |
| Rs. 5001 - 6000 | 52(11.0%) | 89(18.8%) |
| Rs. 6001 - 7000 | 35(7.4%) | 34(7.2%) |
| Rs. 7001 - 8000 | 23(4.9%) | 13(2.7%) |
| Rs. 8001 - 9000 | 13(2.7%) | 4(0.8%) |
| Rs. 9001 - 10000 | 15(3.2%) | 3(0.6%) |
| Rs. 10,001 and above | 24(5.1%) | 5(1.1%) |
| Total | 473 | 473 |
| Average Monthly Income | Rs. 2282.02 | Rs. 2259.35 |

*Source*: Computed from Primary Data
*Note*: Figures in brackets represent columnwise percentages.

As found in Table-3, it was found that there was a significant increase in the lower income respondents earning more in the second year than the first, as more people were pushed from lower to higher income slabs of Rs.3001-4000 and Rs.4001-5000, though the average monthly incomes (lean and peak) for these two years were Rs.2282.02 and Rs.2259.35 respectively. It could be from the fact that

- Prices had gone up,
- More members of the families were deployed in trade,
- Better business strategies and risk management would have raised their income earning capacity.

However, in the second year, the number of respondents who earned Rs.10, 000.00 and above were less than the previous year which might be due to the prices of their goods remaining pitifully low. Yet searing inequalities of income were noticed among them, as some of the respondents were well off with flourishing trade of chains, medicine and others.

This was also not a veritable reflection of the per capita income in India where in 2006-07, it was Rs.29,524 and for Tamil Nadu it was Rs.37,109[1]. The national per capita income for 2007-08 was Rs.33,283 i.e., an increase of 12.7 per cent, according to Central Statistical Organisation (CSO).[2]

### Lean Period Expenditures of 2006-07 and 2007-08 Compared

Monthly lean expenditures had been calculated taking all the daily expenditures of the sample respondents for the lean periods during the study period and presented in Table–4.

**Table 4**
**Monthly Lean Period Expenditures Compared between 2006-07 and 2007-08**

| | *Sample Respondents* | |
|---|---|---|
| *Expenditure Categories* | *2006-07* | *2007-08* |
| Less than Rs. 1000 | 38(8%) | 17(3.6%) |
| Rs. 1001 - 2000 | 197(41.6%) | 133(28.1%) |
| Rs. 2001- 3000 | 166(35.1%) | 185(39.1%) |
| Rs. 3001 - 4000 | 51(10.8%) | 82(17.2%) |
| Rs. 4001- 5000 | 7(1.5) | 29(6.1%) |
| Rs. 5001 - 6000 | 9(1.9%) | 10(2.1%) |
| Rs. 6001- 7000 | 3(0.6%) | 3(0.6%) |
| Rs. 7001 - 8000 | 0(0.0%) | 3(0.6%) |
| Rs. 8001 - 9000 | 0(0.0%) | 0(0.0%) |
| Rs. 9001 - 10000 | 0(0.0%) | 1(0.2%) |
| Rs. 10,001 and above | 2(0.4%) | 10(2.1%) |
| Total | 473 | 473 |
| Average monthly expenditure for lean periods | Rs. 2267.96 | Rs. 2317.96 |

*Source:* Computed from Primary Data
*Note:* Figures in brackets represent columnwise percentages.

It was learnt that majority of the respondents 197 (41.6%) had spent monthly an average of Rs.1001.00 to Rs.2000.00 during the lean season of 2006-07.

But it has been found that the majority of the respondents 185 (39.1%) had higher expenses in the second lean period in range of Rs.2001-3000. This could have been due to the following reasons as stated by them.

- Unabated and higher borrowings by the families for innumerable needs.
- High price rise.
- Bigger size of families.

**Peak Period Expenditures of 2006-07 and 2007-08 Compared**

Peak periods average monthly expenditures of the sample respondents for the study period had been calculated and presented in Table–5. It was found that 196 (41.4%) of them had spent monthly between Rs.1001.00 and Rs.2000.00 during the peak period of 2006-07, while in the second year their number had come down. Similar pattern was also observed in the expenditure category of Rs.2001-3000 for both periods. The average monthly peak period expenditure of the respondents for 2006-07 was Rs.2996.90 and for the next year was Rs.2627.96, showing a marginal decrease of 12.3 per cent.

**Table 5**
**Monthly Peak Period Expenditures Compared between 2006-07 and 2007-08**

| | *Sample Respondents* | |
|---|---|---|
| *Expenditure Categories* | *2006-07* | *2007-08* |
| Less than Rs. 1000 | 32(6.8%) | 18(3.8%) |
| Rs. 1001 - 2000 | 196(41.4%) | 172(36.4%) |
| Rs. 2001 - 3000 | 167(35.3%) | 159(33.6%) |
| Rs. 3001 - 4000 | 56(11.8%) | 69(14.6%) |
| Rs. 4001 - 5000 | 7(1.5%) | 24(5.1%) |
| Rs. 5001 - 6000 | 10(2.1%) | 11(2.3%) |
| Rs. 6001 - 7000 | 3(0.6%) | 7(1.5%) |
| Rs. 7001 - 8000 | 0(0.0%) | 4(0.8%) |
| Rs. 8001 - 9000 | 0(0.0%) | 1(0.2%) |
| Rs. 9001 - 10000 | 0(0.0%) | 1(0.2%) |
| Rs. 10,001 and above | 2(0.4%) | 8(1.7%) |
| Total | 473 | 473 |
| Average monthly peak period expenditure | Rs. 2996.90 | Rs. 2627.96 |

*Source*: Computed from Primary Data

*Note*: Figures in brackets represent columnwise percentages.

**Total Monthly Expenditures (lean and peak) of 2006-07 and 2007-08**

A quick glance at the range of expenditures of the households during the two years gave an overall idea of their expenditure pattern and the households' distribution as given in Table-6.

**Table 6**
**Total Monthly Expenditures (lean and peak) Compared between 2006-07 and 2007-08**

| | *Sample Respondents* | |
|---|---|---|
| *Expenditure Categories* | *2006-07* | *2007-08* |
| Less than Rs. 1000 | 2(0.4%) | 1(0.2%) |
| Rs. 1001 - 2000 | 8(1.7%) | 12(2.5%) |
| Rs. 2001 - 3000 | 44(9.3%) | 51(10.8%) |
| Rs. 3001 - 4000 | 109(23.0%) | 130(27.5%) |
| Rs. 4001 - 5000 | 132(27.9%) | 115(24.3%) |
| Rs. 5001 - 6000 | 88(18.6%) | 70(14.8%) |
| Rs. 6001 - 7000 | 38(8%) | 39(8.2%) |
| Rs. 7001 - 8000 | 20(4.2%) | 22(4.7%) |
| Rs. 8001 - 9000 | 10(2.1%) | 14(3%) |
| Rs. 9001 - 10000 | 4(0.8%) | 6(1.3%) |
| Rs. 10,001 and above | 18(3.8%) | 13(2.7%) |
| Total | 473 | 473 |
| Total average monthly expenditure | Rs.2632.43 | Rs.2472.96 |

*Source*: Computed from Primary Data
*Note*: Figures in brackets represent columnwise percentages.

The above table showed that the majority of the respondents 132 (27.9%) had expenditure in the range of Rs.4001-5000 while in the next year, the majority 130 (27.5%) had lesser expenditure in the range of Rs.3001-4000. Some of the reasons attributed to this difference in the spending habits of the respondents exposed some grim truths. They were;

- Their average monthly income between the first and second years had not changed significantly.
- Secondly, their average monthly expenditures on basic needs too, had not changed drastically.

From Table-7, it was found that there was perfect correlation between lean monthly income of the first year and peak monthly income of the same year (1.00) and less correlation between other seasons of the two years.

**Table 7**
**Paired Samples - Correlations**

| *Pairs* | *Details* | *Correlation* | *Sig.* |
|---|---|---|---|
| Pair 1 | LEANIN1 & LEANIN2 | 0.110 | 0.016 |
| Pair 2 | PEAKIN1 & PEAKINC2 | 0.224 | 0.000 |
| Pair 3 | YEARIN1 & YEARINC2 | 0.231 | 0.000 |
| Pair 4 | LEANINC1 & PEAKINC1 | 1.000 | 0.000 |
| Pair 5 | LEANINC2 &PEAKINC 2 | 0.148 | 0.001 |

*Source*: Computed from Primary Data

**Table 8**
**Paired Samples - Correlations**

| *Pairs* | *Details* | *Correlation* | *Sig.* |
|---|---|---|---|
| Pair 1 | LEANEX1 & LEANEX2 | 0.067 | 0.143 |
| Pair 2 | PEAKEX1 & PEAKEX2 | 0.107 | 0.020 |
| Pair 3 | YEAREX1 & YEAREX2 | 0.101 | 0.029 |
| Pair 4 | LEANEXP1 & PEAKEXP1 | 1.000 | 0.000 |
| Pair 5 | LEANEXP2 & PEAKEXP2 | 0.189 | 0.000 |

*Source*: Computed from Primary Data

From Table-8, the scholar found that there was perfect correlation between lean expenditure of the first year and the peak expenditure of the same year (1.000) and less correlation between other seasonal expenditures of the two years.

**Table 9**
**Correlation between Two Years' Incomes**

| *Year* | *Correlation* | *Year inc - 1* | *Year inc - 2* |
|---|---|---|---|
| Yearin1 | Pearson Correlation | 1 | 0.231(**) |
| | Sig. (2-tailed) | | 0.000 |
| | N | 473 | 473 |
| Yearinc2 | Pearson Correlation | 0.231(**) | 1 |
| | Sig. (2-tailed) | 0.000 | |
| | N | 473 | 473 |

*Source*: Computed from Primary Data
** Correlation is significant at 0.01 level (2-tailed).

The paired t-sample test as depicted in Table-9, showed that the difference in the income between the two years was equal to zero and therefore, there was no significant difference between the two variables. This meant that the income of the sample Narikorava households had not changed significantly between the two reference years.

Since the level of significance was greater than 0.05, it was concluded that there was no difference between the mean incomes of two years as seen in Table-10.

Taking into consideration the average family size of the respondent family as 4.26 persons from the study, it was averred that the per capita income of Narikoravas in Vellore district during 2006-07 was Rs.6428.22 which turned to be 5.6 times less than the district per capita income, 5.7 times less than the State and 4.5 times less than the country as a whole as seen in Table-11. The inevitable conclusion was that they were far below the poverty line by any measure of estimation and they deserve to be treated as the most poverty stricken lot and given all concessions available to SC/ST categories at least.

It was interesting to note, that while the per capita of the State increased by 9.8 per cent and that of the country by 12.7 per cent in the following year, the per capita of Narikoravas decreased by 0.99 per cent a yawning gap indeed. This showed the strange and incisive analysis of the income pattern for this fringe group that languished in filthy conditions and permanently condemned to poverty trap.

From the above table, it was inferred that the Narikoravas were really oblivious of their daily income and expenditure because of their hand-to-mouth existence. Meeting their daily ends was more important than yearly planning. If this was not met, they borrowed hugely throughout the year, so as to keep them in perpetual debt trap unknowingly. Besides, with limited vistas of opportunities to open up their routine business, it was not possible for them to enhance their income and subsequently reduce their expenditure considerably.

Coming to other areas of income generation, the researcher found that borrowings were undertaken more to

**Table 10**
**Results of Paired Samples Test - Income**

| *Years* | *Paired Differences* | | | | | *T* | *df* | *Significance (2-tailed)* |
|---|---|---|---|---|---|---|---|---|
| | | | | *95% Confidence Interval of the Difference* | | | | |
| | *Mean* | *Std. Deviation* | *Std. Error Mean* | *Lower* | *Upper* | | | |
| Year inc1<br>Year inc2 | 45.328 | 4076.3 | 187.4 | -322.9 | 413.630 | 0.242 | 472 | .809 |

*Source*: Computed from Primary Data

fulfil their daily exigencies rather than for enhancement of their business and this too was done more from moneylenders than banks. Besides official banking involved specific identity in their areas of settlement and other formalities for which they were not capable of without any external help. Thus their 'economy' was non-institutional and informal. As a corollary of this predicament, they were unable to join mainstream investment programmes or welfare schemes of the Government for income generation.

**Table 11**
**A Comparative Analysis of Per Capita Incomes**

| *Place* | *2006-07* | *2007-08* | *Percentage Change* |
|---|---|---|---|
| Narikoravas | Rs.6428.22 | Rs.6364.36 | -0.99 |
| Vellore District | Rs.36, 301 | Not available | - |
| Tamil Nadu | Rs.37, 109.00 | Rs.40, 757.00 (Quick Estimate) | +9.8 |
| India | Rs.29, 524.00 | Rs.33, 283.00 (Quick Estimate) | +12.7 |

*Source:* Computed from Primary Data and CSO Report 2009, Ministry of Statistics and Programme Implementation, Govt.of India, New Delhi, at current prices.

Hence it can be concluded that to bring them out of the clutches of penury, direct intervention by the Government or other agencies was necessary. This involved better education among this people as well as specific action programmes by the Government.

*Econometric Analysis*

For the econometric treatment of this thesis, insignificant difference in the income between the two years implied, that one could make use of income of any of these two years for regressing against the possible income enhancing variables by a multi-linear econometric model.

The $R^2$ value was found to be .314, (Table–12) which suggested that only 31.4 per cent of the variation in the dependent variable was being explained by the independent variables included in the model. Therefore, the model fit may be considered to be weak. However, through cross section data the researcher was not be able to capture all the variables that could explain the variation in the dependent variable and therefore, the weak fit was justified. The households had greater difficulty in listing out various aspects that affected their income earning capacity. Similarly, the researcher's cognitive ability to capture all the income influencing variables at the household level was also limited. Therefore, it can be justified that low level of R-square value arising from the analysis of cross-section data was still useful and hence could derive meaningful conclusion from the results coming from the regression analysis.

**Table 12**
**Regression Results of Annual Income Dependent Variable: Annual Income**

| | *Unstandardized Coefficients* | | |
|---|---|---|---|
| *Variables* | *β* | *Std. Error* | *'t' value* |
| constant | 4345.552 | 1346.108 | 3.228 |
| settlement | 75.349 | 38.386 | 1.963 |
| occupation | -174.844 | 1168.699 | -0.150 |
| beads | -129 | 0.397 | -0.325 |
| chains | 0.984 | 0.339 | 2.905 |
| catapults | 5.426E-02 | 0.151 | 0.360 |
| flowers | 0.729 | 0.341 | 2.136 |
| fancy items | 0.126 | 0.183 | 0.688 |
| garlands | -0.926 | 0.955 | -0.973 |
| family size | 733.047 | 78.997 | 9.279 |
| education | -295.321 | 434.318 | -0.680 |
| assets | 898.652 | 999.439 | 0.899 |
| animals | 0.933 | 1.174 | 0.795 |
| birds | 3.044 | 0.584 | 5.214 |
| $R^2$ | 0.314 | | |
| F | 16.195 | | |
| N | 473 | | |

*Source*: computed from Primary Data
a Dependent Variable: yearinc2

*Factors Influencing Household Income:*

1. The variable "settlement" positively and significantly affected the household income. This meant that those households living in the 'healthy' areas were able to earn

more income than those households living in the 'unhealthy' areas. The word 'healthy' was a broader one. It included not only the better availability of basic amenities such as water supply, sanitation, health care facilities, and related facilities but also other income enhancing factors such as, easy access to market and others.

2. The variable "occupation" did not significantly affect the income of the households; however, the sign of the variable provided an interesting intuition. The negative sign implied that the households that took up the 'non-conventional occupations' such as, participating in the regular labour market, were capable of earning more income than those households which were engaged in 'conventional activities' carried out by their community.
3. The "chain" variable (which stood for income from sale of chains) positively and significantly affected their income. This meant that the households that sold chains were capable of earning more income than those who sold beads. "Bead variable" (which stood for income from sale of beads), though positively affected the income, did not affect income, as they were capable of earning more income than those who sold beads. From this it was learnt that people tended to buy readymade chains than beads, which needed dexterous work and time.
4. "Catapult" stood for income derived from selling catapult. Even though selling catapult contributed to increase in income, its contribution to their income was not significant. Selling catapult was a conventional trade strategy of the Narikoravas. Since there was not much demand for this item nowadays, it had become a less income-earning source for these households. One of the reasons for the reduced demand for catapult may be due to the fact that the cultivation of conventional cereals like ragi, kambu and others had come down heavily. Farmers used to buy catapult for chasing away the birds and squirrels that ate the cereals. Since these cereals were not being cultivated

as much as in yesteryears, the demand for catapult had also come down.

5. Of the many items sold by the Narikoravas, was the sale of plastic flowers, which was considered to fetch relatively larger amount of income. Fancy items and garland had become less income generating activities in recent times.
6. While number of years of education of the respondents negatively and insignificantly affected their income generation, and thus disproving the second hypothesis which states that education has enhanced their income. However, the value of assets of the households positively influenced their income but insignificantly as well.
7. The conventional occupations namely, hunting of animals, which supported the livelihoods of these households in the past, had become less income-generating activities at present. However, income from hunting of birds had significantly affected their income.
8. The family size of the households positively and highly significantly affected the income of the households. This might be due to the obvious reason that the households with more family members could earn more because of size of the labour available for generating income, was directly proportional to the size of the households.

## ANALYSIS OF EXPENDITURE

Expenditure showed a slight difference, as there was a decrease in the expenditure from the base year to the next year.

In the case of annual expenditure, there was no significant statistical difference between expenditure between the two reference years, even though the mean annual expenditure differed in absolute terms as seen in Table-13.

The researcher has made an attempt to analyse the expenditure pattern of the households for one year. Table-14, showed that the monthly expenditure on items used by the respondents. It was clear from the table that transport consumed lot of their expenditure followed by wheat and rice.

**Table 13**
**Paired Samples Test**

| *Years* | *Paired Differences* | | | | | *T* | *df* | *Sig. (2-tailed)* |
|---|---|---|---|---|---|---|---|---|
| | | | | *95% Confidence Interval of the Difference* | | | | |
| | *Mean* | *Std. Deviation* | *Std. Error Mean* | *Upper* | *Lower* | | | |
| Year ex 1<br>Year ex 2 | -1.041 | 6265.7 | 289.0 | -1609 | -473.8 | -3.604 | 472 | 0.000 |

*Source*: Computed from Primary Data

**Table 14**
**Basic Statistics of Monthly Expenditure of Households on Various Items (2006-07)**

| *Variables* | *No. of House-holds* | *Mini-mum (Rs.)* | *Maxi-mum (Rs.)* | *Sum* | *Mean (Rs.)* | *Std. Devia-tion* |
|---|---|---|---|---|---|---|
| Ragi, Kambu | 30 | 50.00 | 200.00 | 3450.00 | 115.00 | 54.37 |
| Chicken / Fish | 82 | 50.00 | 300.00 | 9800.00 | 119.51 | 54.86 |
| Vegetables & Fruits | 456 | 25.00 | 500.00 | 64645.00 | 141.77 | 75.69 |
| Oil & Pulses | 358 | 50.00 | 1000.00 | 55880.00 | 156.09 | 104.95 |
| Tobacco / Gutka | 262 | 10.00 | 2500.00 | 51150.00 | 195.22 | 196.94 |
| Liquor | 253 | 20.00 | 3000.00 | 57070.00 | 225.57 | 221.53 |
| Clothing | 219 | 100.00 | 3000.00 | 52250.00 | 238.58 | 265.06 |
| Coffee | 157 | 50.00 | 20000.00 | 56200.00 | 357.96 | 1585.66 |
| Tea | 442 | 20.00 | 3000.00 | 172905.00 | 391.19 | 342.44 |
| Medicine | 212 | 20.00 | 25000.00 | 92860.00 | 438.02 | 2008.44 |
| Education | 134 | 50.00 | 25000.00 | 87400.00 | 652.24 | 2192.63 |
| Rice, Wheat | 472 | 50.00 | 6000.00 | 327325.00 | 693.49 | 441.52 |
| Transport | 471 | 100.00 | 50000.00 | 377430.00 | 801.34 | 2366.12 |

*Source:* Computed from Primary Data.

Although most of the sample respondents were illiterate, yet some of them spent considerable amount of money on the education of their children. It was also shown that there was low correlation between the expenditures of two years as seen in Table-15.

**Table 15**
**Correlation between Two Years' Expenditure**

| *Details* | *Year ex1* | | *Year ex2* |
|---|---|---|---|
| Yearex1 | Pearson Correlation | 1 | 0.001 (**) |
| | Sig. (2-tailed)N | 473 | 0.029 |
| | | | 473 |
| Yearex2 | PearsonCorrelation | 0.001(**) | 1 |
| | Sig. (2-tailed) N | 0.029 | |
| | | 473 | 473 |

*Source*: Computed from Primary Data
** Correlation is significant at 0.01 level (2-tailed).

As seen in Table-16, $R^2$ value was .399, which explains that approximately 40 per cent of variations in the dependent variable is explained by the independent variables of expenditure. Hence the researcher could draw the following conclusions from the regression analysis.

**Table 16**
**Analysis of Expenditure Variables**

| Independent Variables | Coefficients | | 't' value |
|---|---|---|---|
| | B | Std. Error | |
| Constant | -1714.99 | 6380.54 | -0.269 |
| Family size | 20356.30 | 1302.73 | 15.62 |
| Festivals | 0.002 | 0.209 | 0.012 |
| Liquor | -5.52 | 10.89 | -0.507 |
| Food (all items) | 11.61 | 7.82 | 1.48 |
| Tobacco | -1.37 | 25.50 | -0.054 |
| Others (education,clothes, transport) | 6.76 | 13.584 | 0.498 |
| Medicine | 2.26 | 1.03 | 2.19 |
| Marriage | -0.019 | 0.298 | -0.062 |
| Pooja | 0.566 | 0.423 | 1.33 |
| Puberty | -0.360 | 0.526 | -0.686 |
| $R^2$ | 0.399 | | |
| F | 46.70 | | |
| N | 473 | | |

*Source*: Computed from Primary Data
a Dependent Variable: year2exp

### *Factors Influencing Household Expenditures*

1. Size of the family positively and significantly affected the annual expenditure. This was due the obvious reason that more family members would lead to more expenses at the household level.
2. Even though the household expenditure increased due to expenditure on festivals, this increase was not significant.
3. It was strange to notice that there was an inverse relationship between overall expenditure and expenditure on liquor and tobacco. The straightforward or layman's explanation for this phenomenon was that when the expenditure on liquor and tobacco went up, the overall expenditure came down. However, the alternative interpretation was that in those households where the expenditure on liquor and tobacco was high, the overall expenditure in relative terms happened to be low. More precisely, the low expenditure households spent larger amount on liquor and tobacco than high expenditure households. Expenses on food items, positively influenced the overall expenditure but not significantly.

4. Expenditure on other items such as, clothing, positively influenced the overall expenditure but insignificantly as they could not afford new clothes often.
5. The expenses on medicines influenced the overall expenses significantly. This meant that these households very often got sick and spent substantial amount of money on medicines. The alternative interpretation could be that these households preferred to go to private doctors and spend money rather than utilize the services of Government hospitals.
6. Expenses on marriage showed negative sign. This meant that high expenditure groups spent less amount of money on marriage than low expenditure group. Similar kind of pattern emerged with girls attaining puberty also.
7. Expenses on poojas were positively influencing the overall expense but not significantly.

In the above chapter, data related to income and expenditure of the respondents were analysed. The main findings and conclusions are given in the following chapter.

# 7

# SUMMARY, CONCLUSIONS AND POLICY IMPLICATIONS

## SUMMARY

Researchers are to be careful while talking about their research problems. Broader generalizations about gypsies would include that some of them were nomadic while others are settled.

The degrees of marginalisation were different among the different cultural groups due to family situations. Very often the gypsies were confronted with dual conflicts, viz. generational conflicts and cultural conflicts. Generational conflicts were resolved in accordance with customs (for example, shortening of the period of adolescence in the case of early marriage) and cultural conflicts were exacerbated by modernity. Hence they were subject to the demands of a society in the face of which they were vulnerable and ill-prepared. Under these circumstances, new challenges were posed and new questions had to be answered. However, they must be looked upon as people of hope and artisans of renewal in a rapidly changing India.

Hence the pressing need was to have a paradigm shift in the understanding their background and to meet the challenges that involved in making them get into the mainstream of the society at the earliest. "We cannot deny people their aspirations" said Mr. Nandan Nilekani, co-chairman of Indian IT giant Infosys Technologies in an interview by the New York Times' Thomas Friedman in March, 2009[1]. This was true for a group that lived on the fringes of the society They remained wary of initiatives proposed by anyone who tried to penetrate their world. It was only possible to overcome this initial attitude by starting with concrete gestures of solidarity and also via a sharing of experiences and the development of projects on human scale that would encourage participation and support of young Narikoravas.

**Problem Focus**

Narikoravas were considered as one the most backward and depressed classes of the society and ill - treated by other classes of the society even in this 21st century and more in earlier periods. Their social and economic status was very low and pathetic even though they looked happy and contented with their own lifestyle. The vote bank politics of the present-day society has not helped sufficiently to mitigate their distress or make them wriggle out of their vicious circle of poverty. At the same time, they wanted to be liberated from the shackles of penury through Government help and voluntary organizations. Hence it was interesting to study why they were still pegged down to their basic roots in every sphere of living and that goaded the scholar to take this topic for research.

**Objectives**

The objectives of the study were

- to trace the origin and settlement details of the Narikoravas in Vellore district;
- to find out the income sources of the Narikoravas;
- to examine the expenditure and saving patterns of these nomadic people;
- to identify and analyse the impact of social support schemes on Narikoravas;
- to examine the role of education in their upward mobility, and

- to suggest measures to improve the living conditions of these people.

**Hypotheses**

The study had the following hypotheses.

- There is a slow change in the occupation of these people.
- Education has helped them positively in their upward mobility
- Government intervention and involvement of the self- help groups and others have enhanced their income base.

**Methodology**

The research methodology adopted by the researcher included the selection of the study area, collection of data and the tools of analysis. In this explorative study, both primary and secondary data were used even though greater stress was laid on the former.

The primary data were collected from all the 473 households from all the 14 colonies, spanning the entire district of Vellore from April, 2006 to March 2008, by adopting census method. Pre-tested interview schedule was used to collect the required details from the respondents. A set of four enumerators was roped in to assist the researcher to do the data collection for the entire period.

The secondary data, though scanty, were collected from published sources like Vellore District Gazetteers, Tamil Nadu Government Publications, District Collector's Office at Vellore, Tamil Nadu Economic Appraisal, Government of India publications related to the period of study and some leading studies on this community.

Both descriptive and quantitative tools were applied for the analysis of data. Descriptive methods were: simple averages, percentages, graphs and diagrams.

The following quantitative tools were used for analysis: Correlation Method, Regression Analysis, T-test and Basic Econometric Model.

**Scope of the Study**

The study would cover the whole social and economic gamut of the underprivileged Narikorava community in Vellore district. It would be useful to policy makers, sociologists, anthropologists, environmentalists, economists, administrators, academicians and social scientists. It would help them to frame a proper perspective planning for developing the centres wherever they stayed. Proper planning and Government's own initiatives would help this group to join the mainstream of the Indian society. These people must be shown new vistas of opportunities for their livelihood and income generation. Unless their plight was espoused and brought to the limelight through proper media and conscientization of an awakened citizenry, their destiny would still be trapped in the mire of poverty and misery for many more years to come. Hence this study would be an eye-opener in this direction.

**Major Findings**

Vellore district was touted as one the poorest among the 32 districts of Tamil Nadu, which accommodated the second largest number of Narikoravas, scattered throughout the district after Villupuram.

**Demographic Profile in a Nutshell**

- Out of 473 families based in 14 settlements, the largest one was based at Agramcherry with 53 families.
- Their total population in the district was 2017 with a favourable sex ratio of 987:1030. Most of the colonies were miserable by ordinary standards of living.
- Only 41 were females among the total number of 473 respondents. Majority of the respondents were in the age group between 30 and 40.
- It was found that 93.2 per cent of the respondents were illiterates, and only one had passed XII std.
- They all belonged to Wagri caste, spoke a common language known as Wagriboli, a mixture of Marathi and Hindustani with Indo-Aryan roots that has no script. They

are known as Vagrivalas. They were more or less equally divided between Jambalavalas (buffalo-sacrificers) and Nandevals (goat-sacrificers).

- All of them were Hindus by birth and majority of them worshipped Kaliyammal or Meenakshiammal and the rest Samundeeswari.
- Though their plight was worse than that of Scheduled Tribes, they were placed in the Most Backward Caste (MBC) category, while struggling to secure Scheduled Tribe (ST) status, which their contemporaries enjoyed in other southern states.

**Economic Profile in a Nutshell**

- The myth surrounding them as hunters was shattered by the finding that 98.3 per cent of them were hawkers, having a hand-to-mouth existence by selling chains, bangles and other knick-knacks, in the neighbouring towns and pilgrim centres.
- 466 out of 473 families were nuclear and many were with a family size of two or four and most of them had settled in their own places.
- Poor literacy among the respondents was also reflected in the high percentage of children dropping out of school studies, mainly due to migratory reasons. Education had not enhanced their income earning sources.
- Though 66.2 per cent of them could afford only one meal a day, no major disease afflicted their general health condition as 91.1 per cent of them concurred on the same issue.
- Majority of them spent between Rs.2000.00 to Rs.5000.00 for childbirth, which was often conducted in their own houses.
- Marriage ceremony though short, involved huge expenses on the part of the bridegroom who needed to dole out dowry to his bride, which was procured by loan from friends, relatives and moneylenders. Those who

conducted marriages had spent on an average Rs.23,763.00, which often led them to permanent indebtedness.

- Majority of them celebrated Adi festival, followed by Karthikadeepam and their average expenses for the same was Rs.9183.51 per year.
- Most of the respondents lived in their own houses, some of them titled, while others in government built houses that were in dilapidated state in most of the areas.
- Though 43.6 per cent of the respondents owned guns, only 8 of them were regular hunters, who earned a monthly income of Rs.543.33 by hunting (animals and birds) which was less than income earned by hawking.
- Their meagre income goaded them to borrow heavily from relatives and friends (40% from each group) at an exorbitant rate of Rs.6.00 per month for every Rs.100.00 for various needs. Only 13 of them were accustomed to some sort to savings. Existence of Self-Help Group had some positive impact on their earnings.
- In sum, it was found that the fulfilment of their economic problems was more urgent than other issues at stake such as water, housing and healthcare facilities, to live a more dignified life in the society.
- The study had the following hypotheses.
  - There is a slow change in the occupation of these people.
  - Education has helped them positively in their upward mobility
  - Government intervention and involvement of the self- help groups and others have enhanced their income base.

**Income Pattern in Nutshell**

- The economy of the Narikoravas was nearly non-institutional and informal. Insignificant difference in the income between the two years suggested the use of making the data of these two years for regressing against the possible income enhancing variables.

- The R-square value was found to be .314 meaning that only 31 per cent of the variation in the dependent variable was being explained by independent variables that were included in the econometric model, which might be considered weak. This low value of R-square might be justified by the inability of the households to capture all the income influencing variables.
- It was found that there was hardly any significant difference in the in the average monthly incomes of two years.
- While the per capita income of the State had increased by 9.8 per cent and that of the country by 12.7 per cent from 2006-07 to 2007-08, the per capita income of Narikoravas decreased by 0.99 per cent - a shocking tale of their poverty. In fact, their per capita income was 5.6 times less than the district per capita income in 2006-07 and 5.7 times less than the State and 4.45 times less than the county as a whole.
- Area of settlement positively affected the household income, meaning that healthy areas were attributed to better economic infrastructures like water supply, sanitation, health care and others.
- Sale of chains positively and significantly affected the income better than the sale of beads. Hence people tended to buy readymade chains than beads, which were sold in the small towns, pilgrim centres and trains.
- Catapult was a traditional weapon to kill birds, squirrels and other small animals in rural India. Sale of the same increased their income but not significantly.
- Selling plastic flowers was considered to fetch larger amount of income than garland.
- Hunting, the traditional trade of the group was not as lucrative as the sale of knick-knacks because regular hunters, though minuscule in number and dwindling, earned much less than the hawkers.

- While the value of the assets of the households positively affected the income, years of education of the respondents negatively affected their income base.
- It was evident to discern that the family size of the respondents highly affected the income of the households, because more number of hands brought in better income since even small children were potential breadwinners for the family to keep hunger at bay.

**Expenditure Pattern in a Nutshell**

There were varied items of expenditure for these people that were significant to make their life somewhat possible and livable. There was a low correlation between the expenditures of two years as there was no significant difference in the average monthly expenditures of 2 years.

- Size of the family positively and significantly affected the annual expenditure, as more members meant more mouths to feed.
- Expenditure on festivals had not increased significantly.
- There was inverse relationship between overall expenditure and expenditure on tobacco and liquor i.e., low expenditure households spent larger amount on liquor and tobacco, while the high expenditure group spent less amount on these items.
- Expenses on food positively influenced income and expenses on other items like clothing insignificantly influenced overall expenditure because they hardly bought new clothes during the year.
- Though they appeared generally healthy, expenses on medicine cut into their income substantially. Many of them preferred to approach private doctors for treatment.
- Expenses on marriage showed negative sign. This meant that high expenditure group spent less on marriage than the low expenditure group.
- Expenses on their annual poojas were not significant.

## CONCLUSIONS AND POLICY IMPLICATIONS

### Inconsistent Government Policies

One of the primary handicaps the Narikoravas faced today was that they were deprived of central reservations and concessions although in some states they availed these facilities. They had spearheaded the cause for securing ST status in Tamil Nadu and the concessions available under that category. Hence they feel that the State Government had betrayed them. Other communities having a similar nomenclature usurped often concessions now available to them for ST category.

Since they belonged to MBC category, they were not enumerated separately in the decennial census as it was done for the SCs and STs. The correct estimation of their population in the State was not available. Besides their transitory existence, parasitic lifestyle, peculiar behaviour and culture and involvement in socially unacceptable activities like hunting and stealing, posed problems of their integration into the mainstream society.

Narikoravas are considered as non-pastoral nomads, most neglected and discriminated social group in Tamil Nadu whose numbers had surged in recent decades. Their startling numbers might conjure a picture of huge, desperate underclass, trekking long distances for survival. They might be termed as paperless paupers whose multiple woes were hard to disentangle. They had lost their livelihood niche because of drastic changes in transport, industries, production, entertainment and distribution systems. Though very poor and deprived, they were still not facilitated with any constitutional safeguard and concern. Statistics showed that governments were applying a slew of development policies at tandem, which are basically, tailored to SC, ST communities. These development policies were not working because of the cultural and other differences in nomadic communities. It was proved by the present social condition of these communities. Government's tardy policies and half-hearted measures have not yielded concrete results. Hence to stem the tide of hopelessness that threatens to sap the morale of these people, the Government must initiate proactive and target-oriented programmes for them at the earliest, to stall economic insecurity and insecure livelihoods.

**Ways of Integration**

Government of India had set up a commission for the development of these communities in early 2006 and there was then a ray of hope for these people. However, awareness about new initiatives by the Government had to be conveyed among the stakeholders. Their implementation in letter and spirit needed to be pursued vigorously to ensure that the benefits trickle down to the lowest in the pyramid. To cite one example, the much-trumpeted The National Rural Employment Guarantee Act of 2005 (NREGA), renamed as Mahatma Gandhi Rural Employment Guarantee Act, the flagship programme of the present UPA Government, that has promised employment to 4.47 crore rural households and additional income to flowing to wage earners' hamlets to the tune of Rs.18,155 crores, 31.2 million poor families opening accounts in banks and post offices, was revolutionary in its promise of inclusive growth, right to work and dignity of labour. This or other anti- poverty programmes could have increased the purchasing power of these poor folks as a safety net against social and market induced vulnerability. However it had been untouched by them. As Dr. Amartya Sen said that famines are not necessarily famines of deficient production but of deficient purchasing power. Besides, politicians and policy makers all along had suffocated the lot of these deprived people and jettisoned their human rights so as to make these hungry homeless humanity, half-fed victims of state indifference.

How does a nation tackle yawning gulfs between dream and possibility, ability and necessity, hyperbolic manifestoes and practical poll strategies for action to create a more just society? This required social cohesion that should be made real. This again calls for enormous social change in institutions, mindset and relationships. Innovative thinking can produce new social strategies to create the needed paradigm shifts in a vibrant India without borders. Unless India refocuses its policies to address the adverse impact of economic inequality on development and poverty reduction, the poor like Narikoravas and the privileged will continue to live worlds apart. Fruits of prosperity must bring on board everyone without excluding anyone. Injustice perpetuated on them will sooner or later spread simmering discontentment in an unprecedented scale. A disparate and unequal society is most vulnerable when it is faced with unexpected challenges for daily sustenance. *It is therefore in the people's own larger interest to address their issues head on by redoubling our efforts in this direction with necessary and financial resources and tackle poverty holistically.*

**Shelter**

Successive governments have tried to provide housing to this community throughout the district in a limited way ever since 1970s. Most of them abandoned them in course of time because of poor construction. It seems quite illogical and pointless to offer these nomads health, education and other facilities without addressing the question of proper shelter, which is particularly worrisome in most of the settlements, because nomadic lifestyle revolves around being on the move without proper shelter, though this trend is on the wane today. Settlement is the opposite of nomadism, with opposite lifestyles, modified values and customs and redefined social organisation, which define also the bonds that make up their social solidarity. Settlement process, be it partial or permanent, will force them to face up to temporal discipline and community integration. Thus it is a sine qua non factor to end their wandering life.

But this nomadic group was out of the economic development process. *It is high time that schemes like 'Samathuvapuram' may be brought in for this group for permanent settlement, which is one of their ambitions to be included in the mainstream developmental programmes and engage them in suitable economic activities.*

**Their Incomes**

It was heartening to note that their income had remained far below the national average for the two years covered by this study. In 2006-07, the per capita income of India was Rs.29,524.00, registering a growth rate of 8.1 per cent against the previous year . For the next year 2007-08, the per capita income was Rs.33,283.00 (QE) with a growth rate of 12.7 per cent.[2]

The analysis of their per capita income pattern vis-à-vis national average, it was found that they were far below the national average. In fact their per capita income growth had turned out to be negative. This showed that opportunities extended to them for income generation were parsimonious in content and Shylockian in their effect. *Hence specific entrepreneurial skills should be created and arrangement should be made in their neighbourhood to give them jobs to augment their income.*

**Food Security**

Narikoravas are designated as those living below poverty line. Many of them still did not avail ration card that offers some sort of food security and to secure one is long and laborious. "Aam aadmi" (common man) schemes epitomized by the Central Government had failed to touch them. At present, the Centre allocates food grains to the states for the targeted public distribution system as per the poverty estimates, though the states distribute the BPL cards according to survey conducted by the rural development ministry through the state governments.[3] The present UPA government at the Centre has resolved to bring in a National Food Security Act in a bid to provide every hungry family with 25 kg of food grains priced at Rs.3 a kilo. Tamil Nadu has enlarged the scope of Public Distribution System (PDS) to include all vulnerable categories and is making 35 kilograms of food grains available to them per month at Re.1 per kg. Even to get these cards they had to go from pillar to post to get their ration that is promised by the State Government.

Hunger, and equally worse hidden hunger, as experienced by these people, is throwing its tentacles far and wide. The problem of undernourishment, which is widespread and conspicuous among them, is a real blot to India's record. *Hence the State must address the deficiencies in the public distribution system with vim and vigour so as to extricate these people from sinking to the depths of destitution by issuing ration cards to all at the earliest.*

**Social Security**

Unemployment is death by a thousand cuts. Life itself is dependent on gainful work. That is why losing one's job is the beginning of a downward spiral-poverty, indebtedness, disease and suffering follow in quick succession. Unemployment is often seen as an involuntary occurrence and in the case of Narikoravas, social prejudice and unemployability coupled with their attitude of not taking up any work like in farm sector when there is real dearth of workers in this sector these days, added to their woes. That is why there is a need for collective remedy, a system that can help tide people through the dark days of joblessness.

India is one of the more advanced developing economies that barely manage to spend a little of its GDP on social services, which is one of the lowest expenditure in the world. Guy Standing, Professor of Economic Security at the University of Bath in Britain, stated "What is perhaps most worrying in India is that politicians use social protection schemes cynically to boost their political prospects, so that they can show discretionary benevolence, particularly before the elections."[4] Hence social welfare spending that is currently at the rudimentary level needs wider ambit that includes unorgnaised sector as well, so as to emancipate the downtrodden from the clutches of poverty. Indian planners need to spend a little more to cushion the marginalized from the hard shock dealt by fickle economics. They no longer look for yesterday's crutches; they want to run on their own steam. *Hence social security schemes tailored to their conditions should be drawn and implemented forthwith.*

## Education

Education plays a vital role in making them take part in social and political activities. It is a fundamental process for fulfilling personal potential and is necessary for integration within the society. It is a pre-condition for participation in political, social and economic life, on an equal footing with other people. It should encourage rightly critical thinking and responsibility which, in turn, are necessary for building an ever more human society, based on the principles of justice, equality and fraternity. India needs development strategy that straddles the rich and the poor alike.

Narikorava children are second to none in learning in schools that the researcher had visited. Hence the Government must take every step to ensure that dropouts among them are lessened so as to wean them away from their routine trades of hunting, hawking and other non-viable activities by offering scholarships, uniforms, mid-day meals and other concessions and also coaching centres to tutor the school-going kids. The Right of Children to Free and Compulsory Education Bill, 2009 may be touted as landmark legislation in making education a fundamental right of children and an obligation on the part of the Government to impart the same. *With its passage in the Parliament, Government could make a meaningful intervention in imparting universal education at least up to primary level, with the result that a vast number of Narikorava children who were left out of the ambit of learning, could be offered sound education and thus reduce the inequality of opportunity. Besides, eradicating adult illiteracy through continuing education programme is a priority in all the places.*

*Construction of multi-purpose hall, which can be used for Anganvadi, social gathering, educational meeting like tuition for kids, providing skill training by social welfare society, DIC and others should spur alternate livelihood opportunities for these people.*

## Productive Work

Productive work is one of the keys to full integration within the society. There is a lurking danger of total ban on hunting and scrapping of gun licenses for these people. Hence half-hearted sops served on them to garner votes at the hustings such as rice for one rupee, TV, stove and others cannot alleviate their poverty. As Kenneth Galbraith said "What looked one day like the end proved as the next day to have been only the beginning"[5] is their eternal story. Consequently they must be guaranteed the possibility to work in decent conditions even though they are in the unorganised sector. *Rural employment schemes tailored to their needs will plug the financial gaps of these people even though they may not easily take up such works.* Hence correct level playing field must be offered to them for survival. Though there is an intrinsic 'aam aadmi' (common man) component in most of the development strategies of the governments, these people are still dogged by the curse of involuntary unemployment.

There is proven link between youth unemployment and social exclusion. The inability to find employment creates an essence of vulnerability, uselessness and idleness among young people. Occupational training is a major concern insofar as young people must overcome barriers, partly due to the shortcomings of the educational system, which hinder their access to employment. *So the right mix of resources, support and training will transform these youths and create livelihood across the spectrum.*

## Narikoravas and Informal Sector

The Indian economy is passing through a phase of socio-economic upheaval with the onset of globalisation. Rapid urbanization, growing industrialisation, unprecedented rural-urban migration and tremendous population explosion have changed the whole gamut of human life particularly for those who live at the fringes of the society. Narikoravas are part of this informal sector, which is primarily a manifestation of the above mentioned trends, immaturity of employment market and insufficient alternative income generating sources for rural surplus labour. Rising inflation and grinding poverty have further accentuated their plight. Hence they need to be brought under the umbrella of organised labour market. In a massive study "Moving out of Poverty" people claim that they have risen out of poverty through their own initiative and not through handouts.[6]

Hence workfare programmes like Rural Employment Guarantee Scheme, hold considerable potential for providing a form of economic security to these poor families who have able-bodied members left out of formal employment, willing to work in exchange for benefits. Besides, their bargaining power in their sale of their handmade items has to be strengthened with better marketing skills and organization.

Youngsters must be shown prevention initiatives to drag them away from inertia, drugs, alcohol, gambling and other vices. Access to various fundamental rights (decent housing, employment, education and healthcare) can be assisted by the training and deployment of Narikorava Welfare Board set up in the State.

**Mass Media**

Mass media bear a great responsibility in informing public opinion without drawing on stereotypes and generalisations regarding Narikoravas. They must play an objective role in eschewing prejudices against them. *Enlightened electronic media, press, advertisements, articles, debates, editorials and features must unmask the misery of the Narikoravas and espouse their cause more vigorously. It is their social responsibility.*

**Self-Help Groups**

SHGs have done commendable job in reawakening a sense of dignity among most of them particularly among Idaya Nagar women. Excluded, relegated to the margins of humanity and humiliated in their dignity, Narikoravas need such groups to voice their daily struggles and they must be encouraged to start such groups in all the communes where they live. *The researcher reckons that they need to press that advantage home by getting organized in other centres as well to pitch for higher earnings.*

*Besides initiating training programmes, these centres in the district must be availed by them to pitchfork their productive and marketing skills.*

**Banks and Other Financial Institutions**

Banks and other financial institutions must support their cause for income generating schemes by giving liberal loans that support this ethnic group through promotion of micro finance to help them engage in productive activities and thus bolster up their tiny business. With emphasis on disbursement of subsidized loans to prop up local sustainable institutions to serve the poor, this is one of the instruments in creating assets, stabilize income and consumption and protect themselves against risks. Most of them have been ruined by informal sector for micro credit like moneylenders, traders, merchants, relatives and others. If they turn to moneylenders, the lending rates are conservatively estimated at between 30 and 60 per cent. Over and above high interest rates, the poor are loaded with the burden of paying speed money. How does the society expect a below-the-poverty line aspirer to set up an enterprise and successfully run it at profit margins of over 50 per cent? Only then can he repay the interest and the principal.

Today, we need to understand that financial inclusion is critical for achieving inclusive growth in the country. *So formal sector like banks must easily provide start-up capital at low cost and level playing field in the access to such capital. Micro credit may not work wonders but it does help the entrepreneurial poor. The aspirations of these poor people are for larger loans at reasonable interest rates that can raise their income levels, help to build assets, empower these underprivileged, make them breathe an air of confidence and lastly not the least, give them at least some ability to withstand external shocks.*

In fact, there is a success story that is demonstrated by women's SHG of Idaya Nagar colony of Narikoravas in Tirupattur that has shown tangible results with micro credit, which is considered as an anti-poverty tool. *Hence the challenge is to find efficient and reliable ways of providing a richer menu of micro finance to these people to extricate themselves from the vicious circle of poverty. The Government can replicate what it does to the industry and business, at a fraction of the cost, by coming to their aid.*

**Their Struggle to Secure ST Status**

The Centre had reportedly accepted in principle that Narikoravas should be included in the list of STs even as early as 1964, after the State Government had recommended to the Centre that they be included in the ST list. But the required formalities are yet to be completed and the matter is still mired in bureaucratic tangle. *Though the State Department of Adi Dravida Welfare had been extending concessions given to ST to this people, until a few years ago, this was stopped after the Union Government objected to it, stating that the concessions could not be given until the community was included in the ST list by the Parliament.* The Centre was reported to have asked further information to establish the tribal traits of this community. There is a spirited campaign by them to secure this status though hamstrung by state level leadership and organization. *Hence the time has come to stand shoulder to shoulder to secure their due status that is enjoyed by their compatriots in other southern states.*

**A Road map for their Emancipation**

Narikoravas are today the victims of prejudices and social stereotypes. They belong to social group that has fewer opportunities and must face problems of discrimination and inequality regarding educational system, employment, housing and healthcare. According to recent studies conducted in Europe, they belong to the group that is "least desirable as neighbours". This labeling still sticks with the Narikoravs as they are considered modern untouchables. *They were subject to segregation, even to the point of geographical exclusion. This is amply proved by the fact that their housing allotments in the district were at the periphery of mainstream settlement.*

Therefore, a degree of flexibility and humane treatment are needed in approaching the means for encouraging them in the process of genuine integration with equal opportunities in nation-building activities rather being considered as law-breakers. *Government should guarantee rights of full participation in society, which requires new platform for them to operate. Empowerment is better than charity.*

In sum, Narikoravas are one of the most subjugated sections of Tamil Nadu who had been victims of historical dislocations, unconventional occupations, colonial legacy and lastly not the least, social stigma. There may not be any other case in Indian social history where cultural singularity has proven to be a bane to their existence. The emergence of modern, secular institutions including democracy and judiciary has not been beneficial to these people either. Theirs is a classic case of mismatch between tradition and modernity, which has proven very costly in terms of social justice and equality. *There are many unhealed wounds of community segregation, which a caring government must address, to make the Indian growth pattern more inclusive rather than exclusive, because "the dynamics of inclusion is hardly automatic. Solutions need to be carefully designed to correspond to people's concrete lives, based on a prudential evaluation of each situation."*[7] *Hence there is no silver bullet to fight their poverty.*

Tamil Nadu Government had launched a series of initiatives to put welfare schemes in place for them. The policies proposed by the Government in this direction to reduce poverty and inequality, could build positive equity and value. Dr. Amartya Sen has rightly said that "reducing justice is advancing justice" and this has to move in the right direction, for tinkering at the edges to keep them alive with occasional sops must stop. Properly supported, their struggles for basic entitlements can, in turn, become the strongest political initiative to strengthen the democratic fabric. *They too deserve the best value for every rupee spent on their behalf. Hence effective oversight of these programmes is extremely important.*

In the fast track of modern development that is unfolding today in India, they have been kept at the periphery and never included in its orbit. As a result, they continue to remain as a poor, marginalized and powerless community. Unfortunately, their case has not been sufficiently addressed by democratic polity and civil society. *Their closed and inward looking culture has found to be a bane on change and development. The reversal of this perspective is a giant step forward, which urgently needs to be followed with further research, action and advocacy.*

## FOOTNOTES

1. *The Hindu*, March 18, 2009.
2. Computed from Primary Data and CSO Report 2009, Ministry of Statistics and Programme Implementation, Govt.of India, New Delhi, at current prices.
3. *The Times of India*, 28th June 2009,p.6.
4. *The Economist*, June 2009,p.12.
5. Galbraith, Kenneth., *Affluent Society*, Oxford University Press, New York,1998, p.8.
6. *Times of India*, June 28th, 2009,p.8.
7. Pope Benedict XVI, *Caritas in Veritate (Charity in Truth)*, Encyclical Letter, Carmel International Publishing House, Trivandrum, 2009, p.77.

# BIBLIOGRAPHY

## BOOKS


Bagavandas, M., **Chennai Managaril Narikorava Makkal**, Chennai, 1973. (A Book in Tamil language).

Beck, Brenda, **Right and Left: Essays on Dual Symbolic Classification,** Rodney Needham (ed), The University of Chicago Press, 1973.

Benedict XVI, Pope., **Caritas in Veritate (Charity in Truth),** Encyclical Letter, Carmel International Publishing House, Trivandrum, 2009.

Bharathi, Bhakthavatsala., S, **Tamizhaga Pazhangudigal**, Adayalam, Puthanatham, 2007. (A Book in Tamil language).

Bharathi, Bhakthavatsala. S., (ed), **Tamizhagathil Nadodigal,** Vallinam, Lawspet, Puducherry-8, Dec 2003. (A Book in Tamil language).

Bharathi, Bhakthavatsala. S., **Vagri Material Culture**, National Folklore Support Centre, Chennai-34, 2009.

Bhatt S.C and Bhargava Gopal K., (ed), **Land and People of Indian States and Union Territories,** Vol, 25, Kalpaz Publications, New Delhi-52, 2005.

Black, John., **A Dictionary of Economics**, Oxford University Press, New York, 2002.

Bose, N.K., **Some Observations on Nomadic Castes of India,** Man in India 36 (1), 1956.

Brown, Lester R., **Eco-Economy**, Orient Longman Pvt.Ltd, Hyderabad-29, 2004.

Chaman Lal., **Gypsies, Forgotten Children of India,** Publication Division, Ministry of Information and Broadcasting, GOI, New Delhi, 1962.

Das, Veena., **The Oxford Companion to Sociology and Social Anthropology**, Oxford University Press, New Delhi-1, Vol, 1, 2003.

Desai A.R, **Rural Sociology in India,** Popular Prakasam, Bombay, 1969.

D'Souza, Lawrence., **Hakkipikkis,** Kadiyalpayal, Mangalore, 1995.

Dorrich, Hans -Jurgen, Biju Michael, Jean Paul Muller, Helmut Reifeld (ed), **Educating Leaders for Social Transformation,** Don Bosco Verlag, Munchen (Germany), 2008.

Dutt, Bhar., **Vanishing People, Vanishing Livelihoods, India Together,** Bangalore, July, 2003.

Fernandes, Lancy., and Bhakal Satyajit, **The Fractured Society, Awakening,** Mumbai-98, 2002.

Fisher, R.J., **Nomadic Groups in the Caste System**, Man in India, 1981.

Ghodake, N.B., **Encylopaedic Dictionary of Economics,** Vol 5, Mittal Publications, New Delhi-1, 1996.

Guha, B.S., **Indian Aborigines and Who they are - Adivasis,** Government of India Publications, New Delhi 11, 1960.

Haggblade,Steven., Peter B.R.Hazell, Thomas Reardon (ed), **Transforming the Rural Non farm Economy,** Oxford University Press, New Delhi-1, 2008.

Halbar, B.G., **Lambani Economy and Society in Change,** Mittal Publications, New Delhi-35, 1986.

Hatch, William John., **The Land of Pirates of India,** Seeley Service and Co., 1928.

Heredia, Rudolf and Ratnagar F.Shreen, **Mobile and Marginalised Peoples, Perspectives from the Past**, Manohar Publishers and Distributors, New Delhi -2, 2003.

Ingold, T., Hunters., **Pastoralists and Ranchers,** Cambridge, Cambridge University Press, 1980.

Irudayanath, Philo., **Yar Intha Nadodigal?** Vanathi Publications, Chennai-17, 1985. (A book in Tamil language).

Irudyanath, Philo., **Kaatil En Prayanam,** Vanadhi Pdhipagam, Chennai, 1985. (A book in Tamil language).

Irudayanth, Philo., **Kaatil Kanda Marman**, Vanadhi Pdhipagam, Chennai, 1984. (A book in Tamil language).

Irudyanath, Philo., **Kaatil Malarndha Kathaikal,** Vanadhi Pdhipagam, Chennai, 1984. (A book in Tamil language)

Padmabharati, Karasur., **Narikuravar Inavaraviyal,** Tamizhini, Chennai-14, December 2004. (A book in Tamil language).

Kaur,Gunjeet.,(ed.), **Reserve Bank of India Bulletin**, September 2009.

Khazanov, Anatoly M., **"Nomads and the Outside World"**, University of Wisconsin Press, 1994.

Levitas, Ruth., **The Inclusive Society: Social Exclusion and New Labour**, Basingstoke, Macmillan, 1998.

Man R.S., **Hakkipikki, Trapper and Seller**, Anthropological Survey of India Memoir, No.51, Calcutta, 1979.

Mathur, M.L., **Backward Castes Encyclopedia**, Kalpaz Publications, New Delhi-52, 2004.

Mishra, P.K., and Malhotra K.C., (ed.), "Nomads in India", Proceedings of the National Seminar, **Anthropological Survey of India,** Calcutta-16, June, 1982.

Moffatt, Michael., **An Untouchable Community in South India: Structure and Consensus,** Princeton University Press, 1979.

Nayak, Pulin., **Social Exclusion and South Asia,** International Institute for Labour Studies, Cambridge,1994.

Radhakrishnan, Meena., **Dishonoured by History, Criminal Tribes and British Colonial Policy,** Orient Longman Ltd, New Delhi, 2001.

Rajeshwari, R., **"A Study on the Socio-Economic Conditions of Narikuravas Residing at Devarayaneri in Tiruchirappalli District"**, M.A Dissertation, Trichy, 2002.

Omprakash, L.T., and S.Alamelumangai, **Social Exclusion and Poverty; Linkages in India. Millennium Development Goals** (ed), J.Godwin Prem Singh, Allied Publishers Pvt. Ltd., New Delhi-2, 2009.

Pande, G.C., **Indian Tribes, Their Habitat, Society, Economy and Change**, Anmol Publications, New Delhi, 1991.

Paul, Hockings.,(ed.), **Encyclopedia of World Cultures,** Vol III, Boston, (Massachusetts), G.K.Hall & Co, 1992.

Rajagopalan, K.R., Vijaya Tilakan J.S., **Naikoravazkkayil Sadangugalum Poosaikalum,** Chennai, 1972.

Rao, Aparna., and Casmir J. Michael, (ed.), **Nomadism in South Asia**, Oxford University Press, New Delhi-1, 2003.

Randhwa,T.S., **The Last Wanderers: Nomads and Gypsies of India**, Mapin Publishing Pvt.Ltd, Ahamedabad, 1996.

Ruhela, S.P., **Children of Indian Nomads: Studies in Inculturation and Socialization**, Regency Publications, Delhi, 1997.

Sakthivel S., **Tamizhnatu Pazhangudimakkal**, Manikkavasagam Nulagam, Chidambaram, 1980.

Samuelson, Paul A., and William D.Nordhaus, **Economics**, Mc.Graw-Hill Inc New York,1995.

Sankar, M., **Census of Tamil Vagris**, Tamil Nadu Pazhangudi Vagrivel Tozhilar Sangam (TAPVATS), Villupuram, 2008.

Sathyanandan, D.Theodore., **The Problems of Narikorava Community in Tamil Nadu**, The Christian Literature Society, Chennai-7, 2000.

Sen, Amartya., **On Economic Inequality**", Oxford University Press, New Delhi-1, 2008.

Sen, Amartya., **Development as Freedom**, Oxford University Press, New Delhi-1, 2008.

Sen, Amartya., **Poverty and Famines**, Oxford University Press, New Delhi- 1, 2008.

Sen, Amartya., **Social Exciusion: Concept, Application and Scrutiny**, Asian Development Bank, Manila, June 2000.

Sen, Amartya., **The Idea of Justice**, Penguin Books Ltd, London, August 2009.

Sharma, G.L., **Caste, Class and Social Inequality in India**, (Vol.1&2), Mangal Deep Publications, Jaipur-16, 2003.

Shashi, Shayam Singh., **The World of Nomads**, Lotus Press Publications, New Delhi-2, 2006.

Singh, K.S (ed.), **People of India- (Tamil Nadu)**, Vol.XL, Part II,. Affiliate East West Press Pvt. Ltd, Chennai, 1997.

Siromoney, Gift and Giles Lal D., and Livingstone C, **Folklore**, Vol. 14, October 1973.

Sudarsen, V., and Kalam M.A., **The Uprooted, Displacement, Resettlement Development**, Gian Publishing House, New Delhi-2, 1990.

Thurston, Edgar., **Castes and Tribes of Southern India**, Vol IV-K: "Kuruvikkaran", Government Press, Madras, 1969.

Thurston, Edgar., Rangachari K., **Castes and Tribes of Southern India**, Vol. III and IV, C to J, Cosmo Publications, New Delhi, 1975.

Varma, Srinivasa G., **Vagri Boli: An Indo-Aryan Language**, Annamalai University, Annamalai Nagar, 1970.

Varma, Srinivasa G., **Narikoravas Pazhangudi Makkal**, Chidambaram, 1978. (A Book in Tamil language).

Vijayathilakan, J.P, **Studies on Vaagrivala**, Madras Christian College, Dept. of Statistics, Madras, 5 Feb. 1977.

Vijayathilakan.P, **Studies on Vagrivala, A Collection of Papers on the Narikorava People of Tamil Nadu,** Feb,1977.

Werth, Lukas., **"Forgotten People: the Vagri and other Peripatetic Communities of South Asia"**, Conference on Asian Minorities, University of Minnesota, 1996.

**Census of India 2001**, Office of the Register General of India, Government of India Publications, 2001, New Delhi-11.

______**Encyclopedia of Backward Castes;** Commissions, Government of India Report of the Backward Classes Commission, Part 1,(Vo1&2), New Delhi-2, 1980.

______"Gypsies," **Encyclopedia Britannica**, Vol.10, 1969.

______**"Nomads"**, Encyclopedia Britannica, **1964.**

______"Nomadism", **Britannica Concise Encyclopedia**, 1967.

## JOURNALS

Bokil, Milind, "Denotified and Nomadic Tribes: a Perspective", **Economic and Political Weekly**, Jan.12, 2002.

Bokil Milind, "Facing Exclusion: The Nomadic Communities in Western India", **The Indian Journal of Social Work,** Vol, 63, January 2002.

Dhananjayan, A., **Indian Folklore Research Journal,** Vol .4, No.7, Chennai, December 2007.

Hayden, Robert, "The Cultural Ecology of Service Nomads", **The Eastern Anthropologist**, Vol, 32.

Islam Aminul S., "Sociology of Poverty", **Bangladesh e-Journal of Sociology,**Vol.2.No.1, January, 2005.

Kuper, Adam, "Lineage Theory: A Critical Retrospect", **Annual Review of Anthropology,**11, 1982.

Mishra, P.K, "The Nomadic Gadulia Lohars; Their Region of Movement and the Composition of a Band," **The Eastern Anthropologist,** Vol XV, No.3.

Palani, D, "Social Life of Gypsies of Tamil Nadu", **Bulletin, The Institute of Traditional Cultures,** University of Madras, Jan-June, 1976.

"Pastoral Care of Nomads in India", Documentation, 2005, Bhopal.

Peace, R., "Social Exclusion: A Concept in need of Definition?" **Social Policy Journal**, 16 July, 1992.

Verdon Michel, "Where have all their lineages gone? Cattle and descent among the Nuer", **American Anthropologist,** 84, 1982.

Virginius, Xaxa, Tribes as Indigenous People of India, **Economic and Political Weekly,** Dec.18, 1999.

Werth, Lukas, "The Vagri of South India and their Ancestors", **Journal of Indian Anthropological Society, Vol.28,** 1993.

**Economic Survey of India, 2007-08,** Govt. of India, Ministry of Finance, Oxford University Press, New Delhi-1, 2008.

**Economic Survey, 2008-09,** Government of India, Ministry of Finance, Oxford University Press, New Delhi-1, 2009.

**Human Development Report, 2009,** "Overcoming Barriers: Human Mobility and Development", Oxford University Press, New Delhi-1, 2009.

**India, Social Development Report 2008,** Oxford University Press, New Delhi-2, 2008.

**World Economic and Social Survey 2008,** "Overcoming Economic Insecurity", Academic Foundation, New Delhi - 2, 2009.

**World Development Report 2006,** "Equity and Development", A co-publication of The World Bank and Oxford University Press, New York, 2006.

**CSO Report 2009**, Ministry of Statistics and Programme Implementation, Government of India, New Delhi.

**MAGAZINES AND NEWSPAPERS**

**The Hindu,** 7th February, 2008.

**The Hindu,** 21st June, 2009.

**The Hindu,** 9th August, 2009.

**The New Indian Express**, 3rd December, 2009.

**L'Osservatore Romano**, Wednesday, 8 October, 2008, Vatican City.

**Indian Currents**, 12-18th October, 2009.

**Salesian Missions Department**, Direzione Generale Opere Don Bosco, Rome, 2009.

## UNPUBLISHED DISSERTATIONS

Arokiaswamy, A., **Narikuravar Vazhv: Or Ayvu**, ( M.A. Dissertation in Tamil language), Loyola College, Chennai-34, 2000.

Kulandai,A., "**Vagriyargalin Vazhviyal**", ( M.Phil Dissertation in Tamil language), Madurai Kamaraj University, 2007.

## WEBLIOGRAPHY

*wikipedia.org/wiki/Roma_people, pg.1-15*

*www.decanherald.com*

*ww.mtsu.edu/-baustin/gypsies.html*

*www.exnora.org/narikkurava.html*

*www.hindu.com*

*ww.cmi.ac.in/gift/narikorav.htm*

*www.cmi.ac.in/gift/narikorava/nari_ceremonies.htm*

*www.wikipedia.org/wiki/Narikurava*

*www.narikuravawelfare.org/index.html*

*www.answers.com*

*www.findartciles.com*